A JOURNEY

by

Ellen Robin Rubinstein

ISBN: 1-4033-1737-2 (e-book)
ISBN: 1-4033-1738-0 (Paperback)

Library of Congress Control Number: 2002095849

This book is printed on acid free paper.

Printed in the United States of America
Bloomington, IN

1stBooks - rev. 11/01/02

To our youth

Scission

Silence by the lake seems eternal
The autumn air is cool, the night damp
The fire is warming
            yet I feel a chill at my back

Life without you has been confirmed
            again
      by the birth of another son
As tightly as your life is wrapped in hers
So I am alone, sheathed in emptiness

Your infinite distance from here
Your intimate proximity there
      remind me
            again
      that it is over

The stillness now
            quiet, calm
      only the fire crackling
                  with leaves in fall glory
                        and winter approaching
      is juxtaposed to
the stillness then

agonized, vibrating

only a sob interrupting

with summer in full splendor

and fall coming on

And you lay next to me on the white sheet

as the last morning sun lit the room

Your face shimmered through my tears

already less clear

And I left

spent

in solitude

Table of Contents

<u>The Beginning</u>

It was a time of heightened awareness for us all. Most of the volunteers were between the ages of twenty and thirty, a few—myself included—being a year or two younger. In retrospect, I was verging on womanhood, though I still thought of myself and my female peers as girls. My companions included a French girl, a Frenchman, a Swedish girl, two Dutch girls, one Dutchman, three English fellows, one English girl, a few Danes and Swiss who came and went, and a flock of young Americans. I was one of that last group of fifteen who had flown together, planning a seven-month stay. We were all far from home—some having run from something or someone, others taking a break from their normal pace—all of us looking, in the Israeli desert, for something we lacked at home.

The kibbutz members lived in white stucco houses with red tile roofs. Older couples lived in the newer buildings with four apartments per building, two upstairs and two downstairs. Most couples had a bedroom, living room, comfortable (but not large) kitchen, and a toilet room with a shower and sink. In the newer apartments, there was a dining area as well. All apartments were similar, their design being fairly simple and modern.

Younger single members lived in long buildings containing four or five apartments in a row. Each had one fairly large room (bedroom and living space combined), a small kitchen, and a room with a toilet, sink, and shower. The door of each apartment led out to a narrow cement path which ran parallel to the building and continued on to become one of the many paths that wound through the kibbutz leading—once you knew the way—from anywhere to anywhere else.

The area in which the volunteers lived was called the Ulpan. The Hebrew word "ulpan" means an intensive language course. Most volunteers took the offered Hebrew language class for an hour each afternoon. The group and then our living area came to be known as the Ulpan. This consisted of three one-story wooden buildings, forming a U-shape, the two parallel ones about twenty yards apart, with the third building almost connecting them. Two of the buildings contained four rooms; one had three. Each room held either two or three beds, and the same number of dressers. There was a room with a toilet and small sink at one end of the middle building, and a very large outdoor sink at the other end. In the center of the U, a wide shallow hole had been dug, surrounded by stones and bricks, and covered with a large grill: our fireplace and barbeque pit. The whole area was set back about fifteen yards from a narrow blacktop road. Across this road were six or seven 9' x 12' wooden shacks, the residences of the original kibbutz settlers. Each was a single room with one door and one window. These also were used as living space for the volunteers. Nearby was a building housing one sink, one toilet, and two other receptacles, each consisting of a large hole between two raised rectangular footplates, which were about one-and-a-half feet apart on the cement floor—Eastern toilets, the likes of which most of us had never seen before.

A three-minute walk down the road brought one to a modern shower-house, built specifically for the volunteers, with men's and women's areas. Each half had four shower heads in one long tiled area, two modern toilets, a sink, and a large dressing room.

There were a few paved roads in the kibbutz, like the one that led to the shower-house, but they were mainly for the tractor which picked up the garbage, the gardener's tractor towing its cart full of plants, shrubs, and tools, the night patrol car, and an occasional car or pick-up truck belonging to the kibbutz.

Members do not own cars. Several are available, but they are the property of the kibbutz. Members are allotted a certain amount of money annually for gasoline expenses on pleasure trips, and a car may be obtained at any time, as long as no one else has already requested its use. The kibbutz pays for repairs and maintenance of the cars. Along with the economic restrictions of this system comes financial security.

All profits from the kibbutz are pooled, and the members vote on how the money should be spent. The kibbutz at which I worked was agricultural, with many different areas of production. This led to such debates as whether the citrus orchards should get a new tractor in a given year or whether the available funds should be spent on new milking machines for the dairy, the request for a tractor being denied until the following year. It was a democratic system in which both sides were heard and a vote was taken, the majority opinion being upheld. We volunteers had no part in these meetings.

There were, probably unavoidably, some members whose opinions seemed more highly respected than others. The fairness of this within the socialist system may be argued, but those whose voices carried more weight were often better informed than others.

Most jobs were rotated every two or three years. The members who did the buying and selling for the kibbutz would often have to drive quite a bit and be away from the kibbutz most of each day, but this position lasted only a few years. Women held traditionally female jobs; they worked in the kitchen preparing the food for everyone to eat in the large dining hall, and they washed, pressed, and sewed (to repair, not make) clothes for all the members. They cared for the children during their play hours, and cleaned the children's houses. There was occasionally a female member packing fruit in the orchards; there were men working in the dining hall and kitchen every day. Men and women worked in approximately equal percentages in the dairy and with the chickens. High school children, both male and female, had to work one, two, or three hours each day after classes, depending upon age. The girls drove small tractors at times. Women were not given jobs requiring regular use of a tractor, since experience had supposedly shown that constant bouncing could be damaging to the uterus.

The children lived in houses separate from their parents, with about fifteen children of the same age per house. Most of the houses had five large bedrooms; three children slept in each. The rooms were mixed—girls and boys together—but there were separate toilets and shower-rooms. Each house had its own classroom where teachers came to give lessons. There was also a large kitchen where the children ate breakfast and lunch, prepared by the woman in charge of that house. The very young children ate supper there also, while the older ones, about nine years and over, joined their parents in the main dining hall.

An often-heard complaint of those who have never seen the kibbutz system in operation is that the children rarely see their parents. I found this to be untrue. Most of the women work in the kitchen or laundry and sewing area, both of which were close to the children's houses, at the kibbutz where I lived. During the morning, lunch, and afternoon breaks, many mothers would be seen visiting their children. And at almost any time of the day, one could see women walking along the roads and paths of the kibbutz, pushing their babies in strollers.

After their play and rest hour, the children showered, dressed, and went to their parents' apartments. Three-year-olds could be seen, freshly combed, toddling along the paths on their way. There the family members enjoyed each others' company during "aruchat arbah", the four-o'clock meal. This generally consisted of bread, cheese, and fresh vegetables, followed by a home-made cake or some other treat. In the summer months, the members sat outside on the lawns in front of the apartments. Neighbors visited each other; children played games on the grass.

Between seven-thirty and eight, everyone took a leisurely walk to the dining hall, where the members ate supper together. After the meal, some members stayed to watch the television that was in one corner of the dining hall. Others remained to sit and talk. Mothers, and often fathers, would leave soon after dinner and walk with their children back to the children's houses to tuck them in, read to them, and say goodnight. Once or twice a week, movies were shown after dinner. A large screen was unrolled at the front of the dining hall and the chairs were arranged in rows. On those evenings, almost everyone except the youngest children came to see the movie. It was often American, sometimes Italian or French. All had Hebrew subtitles. If there was no movie, we volunteers generally returned to the Ulpan in groups, to sit and talk in each others' rooms or to play guitar and sing. Sometimes we built a bonfire in the large pit between the buildings.

Various members had offered to allow volunteers to visit them in their homes, so that each volunteer could have a "family" during his or her time at the kibbutz. Once each week, on Shabbat, we visited our families. Sundown Friday is the beginning of the Jewish Sabbath, which lasts until sundown Saturday. (The Hebrew calendar day goes from sundown to sundown, rather than beginning and ending at midnight). At around four or five o'clock, we joined our families, the same time that their own children arrived. We sat and talked and shared "aruchat arbah" with them and later went, all together, to dinner.

On Friday night, everyone dressed up. In the dining hall were cloth napkins instead of the usual paper ones, white tablecloths instead of uncovered plastic, and a bottle of Israeli wine on each table.

6

One could sense from the setting and mood that this was a special night, a holiday.

Shabbat was the one day of rest in the week, but many members had to work in order to maintain the smooth functioning of the kibbutz. Cows had to be milked, chickens fed, food prepared, tables cleaned, dishes washed, irrigation pipes moved, and the kibbutz had to be patrolled and guarded at night. These jobs were organized on a rotating schedule, so that each member had to work one Sabbath of every five or six. As volunteers, we were spared that obligation. We foreigners settled into our new surroundings and were welcomed.

<u>The Morning</u>

Upon our arrival in late January, extra hands were needed to pick fruit in the citrus groves. We all dressed in the heavy workboots and thick cotton shirts and shorts we had been given, as well as cotton caps—like a sailor's hat in royal blue, with the brim turned down—or kerchiefs to protect our heads from the strong sun. At ten-to-six in the morning, we walked up the hill to the dining hall for coffee and bread. Two huge stainless steel buckets, holding about six gallons each, were brought to the front of the room. In one shining vessel was steaming coffee; in the other was warm foaming fresh milk. Jason, one of the friendliest of our group, marveled at them.

"Man, have you ever seen so much hot milk in one place?" he asked, shaking his head.

"It's new to me," I responded, inhaling the aroma and delighting in its freshness. We filled our mugs, clicked them together, and toasted the kibbutz. I had never liked coffee, but I followed the customary preparation: 1/3 cup hot coffee, 2/3 cup warm milk, and a generous amount of sugar. It tasted wonderful—hardly like coffee at all. A few minutes later, we went out to the waiting pick-up truck. It had wooden benches and was covered with a canvas shell, to prevent us from being covered and choked with dust. We climbed in and enjoyed a bumpy ride through the desert in the early morning air.

"Whoa!" said Betty, with a big smile. "I almost fell off!"

"It's not easy," I agreed, gripping the edge of the bench and swallowing some dust. "It's a great view, though."

"Yeah," she said, still smiling. Around us stretched waves of tan hills, graceful, calming, unlike any scene in our experience. Ahead lay a small dark patch. Soon, we were able to distinguish the trees of the groves. Ten minutes later, we were surrounded by green, unable to glimpse the barren expanse through which we had just passed.

Upon arriving at the "pardess" (Hebrew for citrus grove), we were each given a large canvas bag which hung down to the thigh when its wide strap was slung over the shoulder. The trees were trimmed so that they would grow wide and not too high; this made for easier picking with limited climbing. The kibbutznik in charge assigned two volunteers to a tree, one picking on each side. We chatted through the branches, sometimes sang, and sometimes worked in silence, breaking it only to check whether our partner was ready to move on to the next tree in the row. When our bags were full, we emptied them into a 5' x 3' crate which had been placed nearby. At the end of the day, the full crates would be moved with a forklift to the location from which they would be loaded onto trucks and shipped.

So each day passed. Sometimes I was paired with my roommate Jen, sometimes with Christine, from France, sometimes with another from my group. We peered between the leaves, picked large yellow fruit to fill our sacks, emptied them, began again, and felt the sun grow hotter and brighter as the morning wore on.

The pardess was so far from the main living area of the kibbutz that it was not worth the time to drive back and forth for breakfast.

Instead, we brought eggs and bread out with us in the morning, and ate in a small shack in a clearing in the middle of the groves. There were two old wooden picnic tables with benches, a gas canister stove and a huge black kettle, along with some frying pans, forks, and other utensils. Several of us went out to pick lemons to make lemonade while others set the tables. Sam cooked.

"What can I get you? Two eggs, over easy, comin' up! Scrambled will be next. How's that lemonade coming along?" He constantly asked questions, responded, and worked. A small, muscular man with a tan, wrinkled face and bright eyes, he was only about forty-five, but aged by the sun. Sam wore a blue kibbutz cap and an almost constant grin. Originally American, Sam had been on the kibbutz for twenty years. As the head of the pardess, he had elected to be the cheerful chef—the expert omelet-maker—at breakfast time. We drank our lemonade, ate Sam's omelets, and went back to picking grapefruit for the next four hours. Then it was time to return to the kibbutz in the bumpy wagon.

When we worked in the "matah" (Hebrew for fruit orchards other than citrus), we also left the dining hall a bit before six in the morning, but rode out in a longer wooden cart drawn by a tractor. This cart had two wooden benches nailed onto it and was completely exposed. As the morning air was cool, most of us wore sweaters or sweatshirts over our cotton work clothes.

Picking fruit in the matah was different from picking in the pardess. The trees grew taller, and the fruit was smaller and more easily bruised. Depending upon the season, we picked apples, pears, plums, or apricots. We worked four to a tree, one on the ground and one on a ladder on either side of the row. We were each given a two-gallon plastic bucket to be hung on a nearby branch. They were exchanged, when full, for empty ones. Then those of us working the tops of the trees climbed back up our eleven-foot ladders to fill them again. Kibbutzniks sorted the fruit by size and color at nearby tables, then packed them into cardboard boxes.

In the morning, the leaves and branches were wet with dew, and the air was cool and full of the smell of earth and fruit. As the sun rose higher, the air quickly warmed, the leaves dried, and we began to perspire. By eight o'clock, it was hot. We piled into the cart and bounced back to the dining hall for breakfast. We washed up briefly, then ate, still in work clothes.

The dining hall was a huge room, built to hold four hundred and fifty people. One of the longer walls was all windows, offering an expansive view of the gently rolling desert; the other walls were painted white. The floor was linoleum and the tables plastic-coated, for easy cleaning. (At the end of each meal, someone would come along with a stainless steel bin on wheels, which held a bucket of hot soapy water, a scrub brush, and a rubber wiper for removing the soapy water from the surfaces. Everyone, including volunteers, had a turn at this job).

At the start of each meal, the hall was divided in two by a long line of tables with food set out. We took our trays, utensils, and napkins at one end, and proceeded down the line, taking our choice of fresh vegetables, breads, cream cheese, yogurt, eggs (hard or soft-boiled), hot cereal, and juice. There were always radishes, scallions, and cucumbers, which one would commonly see chopped up and mixed with the plain thin yogurt, called "lebben", to make a popular breakfast. Two other common foods, which we grew accustomed to eating with bread, were tahina and hummus, spiced pasty sauces make from ground sesame seeds and ground garbanzo beans, respectively. Halvah was also always available, cut into bite-sized cubes.

"What is this stuff?" Jason asked. This Eastern confection, made of mashed sesame seeds and honey, was often eaten after the meal.

"You mean you've never had Halvah?" Dan, another of our group, demanded incredulously. Good-natured, jovial Dan was from New York City. He was fairly short and a bit heavy, with close-cut brown hair and a freckled face. He enjoyed teasing attractive, self-assured Jason, who always took it in stride. Once he had tasted it, Jason never considered himself full without a bit of Halvah.

Breakfast lasted one-half hour. By the time we returned to the orchards, the sun was intense. In summer, we knew we were lucky to be working in the matah, for the leaves kept us partially shaded. Our heads were protected from the sun and rough branches by kerchiefs and caps. We learned not to underestimate the strength of the desert sun, but to accept the heat and continue to work. We learned, sometimes by accident, how far we could lean out from the ladders and how much weight could be put on the branches. Many bright days passed with singing and chatting, sweating and straining, amid visions of delicate brown branches and thousands of green leaves before our eyes.

__Mid-day__

After four more hours of work came lunchtime, which marked the end of the workday for most of the volunteers. We had to work only six hours per day, as opposed to the members' eight. (They returned after lunch for another two hours of work and so were generally finished by two-thirty or three o'clock). Everyone came to the dining hall tired and hungry, and this was a big meal. There were at least two main courses, plus hot soup and bread. The entrees were Western, ranging from stews to pizza, as most of the older members had been raised in Europe. Dessert consisted of fruit, and occasionally cake.

After eating, we lounged in the dining hall. There was no rush to go back to work or to go anywhere. We relaxed in our dirty sweaty workclothes and talked. Reading the newspaper—English versions of the most popular Israeli papers were available—was a common post-meal pastime. There were several; the two largest parties, left and right wing, published their own papers. Discussing politics is common practice in many countries, wherever people are gathered for business or social reasons. But never have I seen anything to compare with the intensity with which the kibbutzniks endlessly discussed the politics regarding their country.

For thousands of years, the Jews and their Arab neighbors had been battling each other, neither letting up in their fierce resolve to remain where they were. The controversy was intense long before

1948, when the state of Israel was formally established. And although it had now existed for twenty-five years, with its own political parties and government and international relations, the antagonism was not calmed. Even during times of no war, there was no peace.

The fact of living on a political precipice was keenly felt, even on this remote desert kibbutz. After high school, at the age of eighteen, young kibbutzniks went away, for two years, to the army. They were our friends and peers, but hardly a word was spoken about the army when they were home for Shabbat or vacation. Their personalities varied from brash to silly to quiet, as in any group. But in their seriousness regarding the army, all were the same. The women, though not trained for combat as were the men, held positions of responsibility in communications, and preparations such as parachute folding.

At certain times they listened attentively to the radio, apparently waiting to hear some codes which we knew of but knew nothing about. Their country was on the line, their lives were on the line, constantly. The Israel which shocked the world when it fought back an Arab attack in six days in June of 1967 was intensely aware of its position, and prepared to fight for its life. High tension was not felt in the course of the day's events, but the undercurrent was there, always.

In the spring and summer of 1973, the fronts were quiet and had been so for several years. We were even taken on a trip to visit the bunkers closest to the Suez Canal, which had been the center of conflict in the 1967 war. It was a relatively calm time; we sat back and discussed the less savage aspects of politics after our meals.

<u>The Afternoon</u>

After lunch, we showered. I remember summer days when the heat was so intense that by the time we had walked back to the Ulpan from the shower-house, damp towels in hand, we were soaked with perspiration.

The volunteers generally spent the next few hours together; that is, in one large group or a few smaller ones. We often sat on the lawn to one side of the Ulpan, writing letters and talking. Letter-writing was a common activity, since all of us were traveling and far from home. It was during this time, too, that we told each other about our families, friends and countries. Our eyes were opened to different attitudes and upbringings. Among other things, I learned to roll Dutch tobacco (though I didn't smoke) and added the recognition of a Basque accent to my fairly substantial knowledge of French.

It was thanks to my ability to speak that language that my friendship with Christine was facilitated. She was French, spoke no English, and had come alone to the kibbutz. We liked each other immediately, and went on to share many enjoyable experiences.

Learning simple phrases in other languages, such as how to ask for a cigarette in Swedish—one of the volunteer Ingrid's favorite questions—or how to name the colors of a traffic light in German, was not very practical, but those afternoons were precious.

"Die verkersample ist rod oder groen oder gelb," I recited from Franz's textbook. ("The traffic light is red or green or yellow.") I practiced to get it right, wanting to learn something that one of my new friends could say with ease. He was Swiss-German, studying English; we helped each other.

"Alle landen van het wereld," I repeated after Theo (pronounced Tay′-o), in Dutch. He was reading from his passport, from the section regarding restrictions on foreign travel. There were none for citizens of the Netherlands. How wonderful, I thought, not to have the politics of your country hold you back from exploring wherever you choose. Theo then explained that he had come to the kibbutz out of political interest; he wanted to see a socialist system in practice. Looking at his passport, I repeated in Dutch, with wonder, "All the countries of the world."

The glow through those days was our growing awareness of variety in the world, and comprehension of the closeness we could share.

With time, of course, personalities became more distinct, accents became less noticeable, and we knew each other by much more than nationality. We volunteers became a community in ourselves. One of the strongest emotional blows came, in fact, with the departure—months after our arrival—of a good friend from the Ulpan. I was struck by the realization that our existence together, while young and strong and still developing, was only temporary. I would observe its continual erosion as, one by one, each returned to his or her distant home. But that will come later.

Those delightful afternoons were spent writing, reading, and studying each other, on the bright green grass under tall trees by the

16

Ulpan. We learned that one does not lie out in the Israeli sun to become tan. Enough time was unavoidably spent in the sun, during work hours, to darken our skin; relaxing—for which we were fortunate to have the opportunity each afternoon—was done in the shade.

E. R. Rubinstein

The Sunset

Later in the afternoon, we often took walks to watch the sun set. In two's or three's or occasionally a large group, we wandered west toward the fields to see the huge red orb slip below the horizon. Since most of us had grown up in the midst of trees and buildings and telephone lines, we were fascinated by the sharp outline of the burning scarlet circle poised on the interface of stark land and gray sky. Equally fascinating was the fact that we could count to ten from that point until the sun was gone; no tricks, no golden reflections off glittering window-glass, no peeking through branches or hiding behind houses. It was there, it dropped, and was gone.

One evening during our first month, several of us decided to have a sort of sunset picnic, eating watermelon while watching from a vantage point. Betty, her roommate Lisa, Jason, Dan, Stan, and I were the Americans usually ready to explore. We were often joined, as we were that evening, by Theo and a young female kibbutznik.

Mara had completed her army service and worked full time at the kibbutz. She was only a bit older than most of the volunteers and liked spending time with us. Energetic and friendly, she danced with us after dinner on Shabbat, occasionally accompanied us on walks, and invited us to visit at her apartment.

Theo, one of the most sociable volunteers, was striking due to his height—several inches over six feet—broad shoulders yet slim build, and sharp gray-green eyes. As he always showed an interest in

18

others, many of us were attracted to his emotional sensibilities. He was easily absorbed in discussions, and eager to share stories and descriptions of his friends in the Netherlands. With graceful gestures of his long hands, he would relate these, in detail, occasionally pausing to brush his fine blond bangs from before his eyes. I found him captivating and kind.

That evening, after a long walk out to one of the fields, all of us pushed and lifted to rearrange some stacked bales of hay into a step formation against the rest, then climbed on top of the large rectangular heap. We had brought several watermelons from the small patch the kibbutz kept for its members (and allowed us to share). Earlier that day, after work, Mara had borrowed a small tractor with trailer and taken me and Theo out to pick the melons. It was my first opportunity (of two) to drive a tractor, which was a bit nerve-wracking but exhilarating. The melons were round, eight or nine inches in diameter, with thinner rinds than the larger oval ones we had at home.

Twenty feet above the ground, we watched the sun go down over the desert and disappear behind dusty hills. In the fading light, we sat perched upon our lookout, eating delicious red melon and blissfully jabbering away. It was sweet to survey the land that was, for a time, ours to live on, to work, to wander.

<u>The Evening</u>

The evening meal was similar to lunch in offering, but everyone arrived showered and in clean clothes. Afterward, a group or two of volunteers would head back to the Ulpan to lounge together. Betty often made tea, and we sipped it, milling around and enjoying the clear night air.

Having become more familiar with each other after a couple of weeks, we gathered on a cool winter night in the room shared by Theo, Reggie (an Englishman), and Bruce (an American who had come alone). All three had arrived about a month before our group. A party was in the air that night. Rather than talking in small groups then breaking up early to write letters or read, about twenty of us crowded into that one room to sing.

Perhaps it was the beginning of a community feeling we were celebrating. We were at that delicious precipitous stage of knowing each other a little bit and wanting to know more, of being barely comfortably adjusted to a new environment and relishing experiences to come. The excitement showed in the faces I saw as I looked around, as well as in my own laughter which, for the first time since our appearance in this strange place, I felt safe enough to let free.

Reggie had a guitar which he pulled out and tuned.

"So, how about some oldies? We can all get together on that, I should think." We sang old soft rock songs; we sang currently popular rock songs. We also sang some country and folk songs that everyone knew. Our voices were tentative at first but grew more bold, as we became accustomed to the sound of ourselves and each other. Although we had no alcohol, there was a sense of intoxication.

I recall smiles and images of singing faces crowded together. I remember that Theo, for lack of another seat, sat on a small (unlit) kerosene heater—the kind they gave us to warm our rooms. His long thin legs looked funny, like a grasshopper's; he was so tall and the heater was only two feet high. On his large feet he wore solid leather sandals that laced together, with wool socks underneath. I thought it unusual but later learned it was a common Dutch style, wearing sandals through most of the year, with heavy socks for warmth.

We sang and joked. I even told an old French story that I'd read for a literature class, although I was a bit self-conscious.

"There was a woman whose husband had died. She was terribly sad and wore black all the time. She swore she would never love another man until the river changed its course. A few weeks later, a neighbor heard some noises at night and went to find out what the sound was. The widow was digging in the woods, to force a new path for the stream that flowed by her house."

Though others seemed merely amused, I thought it very funny and laughed without care, allowing myself the luxurious relief of abandonment in the comfort of our young, accepting society. Theo later told me that he fell in love with me that night, though all I noticed was his serious observation of me. It must have been a flattering circumstance: the view of a young woman in unfamiliar surroundings allowing herself to be embraced in the arms of new warmth and companionship.

There were still evenings when we sat around and just chatted, but group get-togethers including singing became more commonplace. We often had two guitar players, and I sometimes played my flute. I improvised, which was new to me, and did so before a group of friends rather than in my room, which would have been my choice a few months earlier.

The Night

At the end of each evening, we wished each other a good night and parted to go to our own rooms. Even Cal, an anomaly in our American group as he seemed to have a perpetual sneer for the world, would make the effort to say he'd see us in the morning. Private friendships, let me call them, were already formed. They were noticeable in that small groups or pairs of volunteers could be found talking outside, after the large group had broken up. Sometimes they were roommates, on their way to their rooms. Sometimes they were couples, romance on their minds, who wanted a few minutes to look at each other. (That, at least, was my naive perception at the time. I later learned that several volunteers were already having sex).

Betty and her roommate Lisa—thin, flirtatious, smiley, and dimpled—were already good friends, as were Dan and Stan. Theo and Reggie were usually talking at the end of the evening, as Jen and I walked amiably back to our room. Jason often joked around with Lisa as the rest of us wandered off. From things I later heard, it seemed they spent some of those nights together.

Theo often talked for a while with the pretty Swedish volunteer Ingrid, before going to bed. She would advertise her large blue eyes by peering up through her long, curved lashes at him or whoever she was with. Often shaking her blond curls a bit, she would draw one's eye to her short, shiny hair. She told us she had hiked over snow-covered mountains in her clogs, and other such nonsense. Christine was very fond of Ingrid and spent a lot of time with her but complained to me that she lied. Still, there was something childlike and charming about Ingrid, part of which was her eagerness for attention and affection.

When Theo conversed with her, he always ended with a fatherly kiss on the forehead, which she would tilt her head slightly to receive. As I felt drawn to him, I was curious. Yet I recognized, somehow, that his affection for her was nothing that would ever cause me jealousy. As I came to know Theo, I understood better what I had sensed; he really did have a paternal attitude toward that frivolous, needy girl. He grew discouraged, though, after learning that she had spent a night with Reggie. He knew neither of them meant anything to the other. When she told him they'd had sex again in the morning, Theo was disheartened. Perhaps Ingrid was hoping he would be jealous, but all she got was criticism for wanting to live an empty life. There was rarely interaction between Theo and her after that.

Once in bed—after a walk with our flashlights to the washroom— the night was quiet. There were no trains clattering by, no jet planes zooming overhead, no sounds of traffic or distant car horns. The only disturbance was the sporadic clanging of metal. This resounding noise occurred for a few minutes several times a night, mostly in the summer, and often awakened me. It was the bulls, banging their chains against the bars of their prison.

The Lesson

For the first few days, the American group had been walked around the kibbutz by Reuben, the man who would run our Ulpan (the intensive Hebrew course). He was an Egyptian Jew, bright, friendly, and almost clown-like in his bright-eyed, grinning eagerness to be helpful. In his early fifties, Reuben was in excellent physical condition, and a man of serious determination and commitment—a fact of soul binding together all the kibbutz founders.

He had three sons. The younger two were dark-eyed with curly black hair—handsome, sturdy evidence of their parents' Egyptian origin. The oldest, Aaron (pronounced Ah-rone'), was a strong-faced blond with sharp blue eyes (who, we soon learned, was capable of being irresponsible for the sake of being playful). He had been adopted by Reuben and his wife as a baby, the son of a close friend who had died. Their mother was a short, sweet, gossipy woman who seemed constantly overly concerned with everyone's happiness.

Both older sons, Jonathan (pronounced Yo-na-tan) and Aaron, were in the army. Jonathan was a member of the paratroopers, a select group rigorously trained for special missions. He always wore a long gold chain with a small gold pendant molded into the shape of a parachute. Not a word was ever heard of their army work; all we knew was that they came and went. They had been out of high school for two or three years and were full-time soldiers, home at the kibbutz only on leave or for holidays. We therefore did not have the opportunity to get to know them very well.

Only a few of the young kibbutzniks socialized to a great extent with the volunteers. The more outgoing, curious, and perhaps restless ones enjoyed spending their time with us. Aaron was one, as was Mara.

Reuben's dark-haired sons spent most of the time they had at the kibbutz with their family. But Jonathan must have spent a lot of his free time with at least one volunteer before we arrived; he had a girlfriend who became his fiancée during my months there. She had arrived at the kibbutz a couple of years earlier, one of a group of American volunteers like ours. Her name was Janie, and she had red hair. Aside from those facts and the lack of complete fullness of vowels and depth of gutterals in her Hebrew pronunciation, she seemed to be a kibbutznik. Janie was quite willing to discuss her past in the States and her present in Israel; she was clear on the point that she intended to marry Jonathan and remain on the kibbutz for the rest of her life. When we spoke, she struck me as very serious, almost demonstrating that reserve that I, as an outsider, felt when confronted with the deep gaze and surface questions of many of the members.

I do not know if Janie and Jonathan were living together at that time; they may well have been. The kibbutz was a liberal one in many respects. Some customs were followed, though not in strict form; religion was rarely mentioned. Jewish holidays were lightly observed, in a manner that would have been considered totally inappropriate by an Orthodox Jew. Passover, for instance, was celebrated with white tablecloths, special wine, and a short Seder, the traditional Passover service which is read at the table before and after the meal. There was unleavened bread—matzoh—which was blessed and eaten. But leavened bread was also available at the main dining room table. Coming from a Conservative Jewish background (somewhere between Orthodox and Reformed, tending toward the latter), I was shocked. I had expected to see only matzoh and no bread served for the eight days the holiday lasted.

Strict teachings would not have allowed a couple to live together before marriage, but it was fairly common at this kibbutz. It was, however, a carefully monitored and well-deserved situation when it did occur among the members. When two young members had shown a long-term (at least a year) romantic interest in each other, and when they seemed to be on the road to a life together, they were encouraged to live together before they married. The members as a group (as well as availability of apartments) made these decisions. In a sense, all children of the kibbutz were children of all the members and were subject to the same parental scrutiny.

The attitude of the members toward the volunteers was more "laissez-faire". Within this group, there were many romances, occasionally resulting in the kibbutz gaining two members. Some lasted for months, after which the couples left the kibbutz together to continue their joined lives elsewhere. Many others were short-lived. There were also brief pairings for the purpose of convenient sex, which I tended to hear about after they had ended. The kibbutzniks had a fairly good idea of what went on among the volunteers and were

27

tolerant unless a problem arose. One such "problem", prior to our arrival, was the sexual involvement of a kibbutz high school girl with an American volunteer. He left the kibbutz a few months after the start of the relationship, which resulted in a much more protective attitude on the part of the members toward their children.

Several older members, like Reuben, Sam, and Hannah—who helped with our laundry and secured any items we needed—were close to the volunteers and worked or talked with us daily, treating us as though we belonged. But most kept to themselves. In conversation, I sensed they were subtly radiating the point that I was not one of them. A volunteer could, however, reach a position of responsibility if he or she stayed for a long time. By showing reliability and, more importantly, a desire to stay and become part of the kibbutz, one could be welcomed into the fold.

Janie, Jonathan's fiancée, had attained this state. She had been just like me and was now one of them. She had found her man, her family, her place in the world.

One day, something strange happened. Members were seen talking urgently together here and there. We saw their disturbed faces and sensed trouble around us, though the volunteers would not be informed directly. By the end of the day we learned that Jonathan had been killed in a horrible accident. The story was that he had been driving a truck full of explosives for the army. We heard that there had been a problem with the steering, that he had stayed in the truck too long, desperately trying to prevent it from overturning. The general supposition was that he had been planning to do what he could to right its course and then jump out, if necessary. Maybe he had been found in the vehicle, or a few feet from it, not having jumped soon enough or far enough. We never knew. The details we did get were mainly from our kibbutz brothers and sisters, who got the news from their older brothers and sisters in the army.

It hit everyone very hard. The kibbutz family had lost a son, a son on one of the founders. They would have mourned any lost child, of course, but Reuben was particularly well-loved and highly regarded. For us, the volunteers, this particular death came close to home. Jonathan had been the older son, by birth, of the man who taught us Hebrew, who taught us about the kibbutz, who was always ready with a smile or story or opinion, if not an answer. He had been the fiancé of a young American who had arrived as we had, only a few years earlier. And he had been young, strong, and friendly, one of the many people of our age but of another culture whom we had become accustomed to seeing on weekends.

The impact forced us to focus more sharply on the barbed wire that surrounded the kibbutz, to hear more clearly the Jeep that patrolled its perimeter each night, and to remember more precisely where we were.

The Sights

The agency which had organized the American group's trip, and to which we had each paid a sum greater than the cost of the airfare, gave money to the kibbutz. Some of that donation funded several bus excursions, on which Reuben took us to see a variety of amazing sights. Although the benefits were intended for our group only, Theo and Christine always came along. They were close with several of us Americans, and Reuben saw no reason to refuse their request to accompany us, considering their interest in the trips.

We floated together in the Dead Sea, surprised at the remarkable buoyancy of which we had heard. We noted the salt crystals along the shore and gratefully rinsed the irritating, rapidly drying liquid from our skin at the available outdoor fresh-water showers.

Once walking along the top of the Golan Heights, in soft grass, shaded by small trees, we saw remnants of low structures, formerly Lebanese guard buildings.

"But why were they destroyed?" I wanted to know. Reuben considered a moment before responding.

"To show, ah, that they could not be returned." Was that necessary, we wondered. Then we looked down at the kibbutz below. Snipers used to shoot at innocent members from where we stood. It was too easy from there. Israel had judged this rise too dangerous to be held in any hands but its own.

Another day, we walked for several hot hours through a "wadi", or dried stream bed, to reach a monastery. Our trek was on pebbles and sand, with light tan walls on either side. We passed an oasis consisting of about a dozen date palms but little water. On we trudged, through air baked dry by the sun. At the end, we were rewarded with a tour through an extensive, dark, and relatively cool monastery built, of the same tan stone, into the side of a hill. It would have been camouflaged but for all the right angles where walls met roofs.

The scent of incense hung heavily in the air; in one room a robed man paced, swinging a smoking brass censer. Another sat silently in an adjacent room, meditating. Our guide told us that he had been there for twenty years but was not yet considered wholly committed. The tan walls were bare, and there were no electric lights.

Exiting to the desert sunlight was jolting. We had the long walk back to consider the alternative approach to living to which we had just been exposed.

Another trip was to see the "Hexagon Pool", where the vertical rocks surrounding a small, deep, and very clear body of water were all formed with hexagonal cross-sections. With long, massive gray stones, about a foot in diameter, tightly packed against each other, the structure at first appeared artificial. The columns of rocks ended at varying heights; we were easily able to climb over them to choose the ones we wanted to sit on, or leave our towels on before swimming. It was a geologically stunning sight, as well as a welcome spot to cool off in the relentless sun.

We were all exposed to these new fascinations together—Theo, Christine, Betty, Dan, Jen, and the other Americans in our group. It gave us much to digest, much to share.

The Lark

One of those glorious early spring days was drawing to a close. The solid blue of the sky was interrupted only by a few bright clouds stretched thin, parallel to the horizon. As they changed from white to pink with the reddening sun, the breeze was mild, the air delicious.

A group of us spent the hour after dinner in Theo and Reggie's room. Reggie and I were the center of attention; he played his guitar, and I my flute. The others sang along with the familiar songs we played. By this time, a standard repertoire had been developed, including folk songs and rock songs known to both of us, as well as to the majority of other volunteers. Once we had exhausted most of the songs we knew, people started to leave.

Theo and Reggie sat talking as I played random snatches of songs on my flute for my own amusement. Eventually, I tired of it and put my flute away. We three, the only ones left, talked for a while, then walked out onto the wooden porch and stood quietly, looking up at the moon. The air was clear and calm and pleasantly cool. We lingered, enjoying the evening and the company, none wanting to alter the moment.

"Let's go for a walk," Theo suggested.

"It sounds great," I responded. I had been enjoying his company more and more, and was glad for any opportunity to prolong our contact. "It really is time to go to sleep, though," I reluctantly added. The early hour at which we had to rise was still a bit difficult to manage, and we all had six hours of physical labor ahead, the next day.

Reggie offered,

"Well, why don't we just sleep outside?"

"My sleeping bag is ready," Theo grinned. He slept in it every night, on his mattress, to avoid having to make his bed. Reggie and I laughed.

"Where should we go?" I asked.

"Let's go out to one of the fields," said Reggie, "out past the refet (dairy)." Theo and I agreed.

"I'll be back in a minute," I said.

Thus was formed the plan to take our sleeping bags and wander out to the darkening fields until we found an appropriate spot to lay them down and spend the night.

Quietly, so as not to awaken my roommate, I took my sleeping bag then met Theo and Reggie at their door. We stepped softly out of the Ulpan toward the refet, feeling like conspirators. I forgot about the need for sleep. Once we had passed the bulls' pens and approached the open fields, the vague guilt faded. An exciting sense of freedom subtly grew within us. Soon we were chatting happily and walking a bit more quickly.

The half-moon was bright, and we had no trouble following the pale dirt road which separated the fields. Night was almost upon us: the sky was a dark grayish-blue, and the first few stars were just noticeable. We walked for close to half an hour before the conversation turned to our purpose.

We decided to march into the alfalfa field on our right. It was filled with soft leafy green plants, close to two feet high, like deep clover. We waded through our chosen carpet until we could no longer see the road, then unrolled our sleeping bags, putting the head ends together. We lay down on top of our open bags, nestled deep in alfalfa, and talked for a while longer. There were endless topics to be discussed, and questions to be asked and answered, regarding our lives at home, our life at the kibbutz, other travel experiences, the political situation in Israel, our jobs, our new friends, our old friends, and more. Finally, the moon set and, despite the stars, we had difficulty seeing each others' faces. Tired from the long day, we were finally calmed enough to say goodnight and sleep.

I saw many tiny green leaves against a pale sky, and realized where I was. The cool morning air bathed my face. As I turned toward Theo and Reggie, I heard a faraway hum. I thought it was an airplane. By the time we had made eye contact, the sound had grown loud enough to cause us to sit up and look around. There was no plane to be seen in the sky, and the hum had become a rumble. We scanned the extensive field with our worried, sleepy eyes, and made out an object in the distance. We squinted and stared as the huge shape approached. The sudden realization that it was a thresher was immediately followed by our jumping up and grabbing our sleeping bags. "Oh no!" I breathed.

"Come on!" said Theo.

"Let's get the hell out of here!" yelled Reggie.

It was moving very quickly, now only about fifty feet away and coming directly toward us. Terrified, with pounding hearts, we ran.

Over our shoulders, we saw the giant machine more clearly: an enormous, rolling cylinder in front, formed of two hoops of green metal connected by many sharp horizontal blades, powered by a large green tractor with a glass-enclosed booth on top. As we ran out of its horrible path, still staring at the slicing beast, we saw a furious kibbutznik leaning out of the booth, screaming at us. We turned away and ran harder, unable to avoid noticing the flattened wake he had left behind.

We ran all the way to the road, then stopped to roll up our sleeping bags, which until then had been clutched in our sweaty hands and dragged. Once this was done, we looked at each other openly, seriously, still breathing heavily. None of us knew who the driver of the thresher had been, but we were sure he knew us.

It was still early enough to get to work on time. Shaken, and with a sense of impending doom, we walked the rest of the way back to the Ulpan, changed clothes, and left for our respective jobs: Theo to the refet to feed the cows, Reggie to the fields to move irrigation pipes, and I to the pardess to pick oranges.

When we went in for lunch, I saw them. We three sat together, feeling even more like guilty conspirators, sensing the members' eyes upon us, waiting for the blow.

The blow never came. There was no reprimand through Reuben, no angry kibbutznik pulling us off to the side of the dining hall to tell us that we were foolish and irresponsible, no notice of any sort given us regarding that morning's events. Like a wise parent, the member who had caught us—or the body of members, as it is unlikely that he would have kept the incident to himself—apparently thought our terror had been punishment enough. Like good children, we were worthy of that trust. We never did such a thing again.

<u>The Community</u>

Every Friday night, tablecloths covered the dining room tables, and there was a bottle of sweet Israeli wine on each one. There was no service, no blessing spoken, but the Sabbath was celebrated. This night was the highlight of the week, to be followed by a day of rest. It was a religious observance without the ceremony usually associated with religion. These people, the members, were liberal in their attitudes and did not wish to constrain themselves by ritual. Yet they were deeply Jewish, tied to their religion and each other by suffering, hoping, striving, and hard work. They lived their religion; their culture, habits, and day-to-day activities expressed their Judaism.

Other than the wine, there were no special foods. But after dinner, everyone went to the Moadon (Mo-ah-done'), the large community living room. It was a spacious hall with a stereo system, many couches and chairs, as well as a sink, refrigerator, and counter at one end. The center of the room was open: this was the dancing area. There was no alcohol, only juice and punch. (In fact, many of the wine bottles from dinner remained unopened on the tables). Music was played, and many members danced. Some preferred to sit and chat, taking this most relaxing opportunity to socialize. The members with young children walked them back to the children's houses, often staying to tuck them into bed and talk or read to them for a while, before joining the other adults in the Moadon. Such a party was held each week, further binding an already close community.

We, the volunteers, had our own Moadon. Though we were welcome at the members' building, it was not as much fun. Ours was a large rectangular structure, approximately the same size as the members' Moadon, but with fewer amenities. It was not as well lighted and was relatively bare; there were some folding tables and folding chairs. Most importantly, we had a stereo system, and we danced for hours every Shabbat. Some of the younger kibbutzniks, usually those who were in the army or attending university, joined us. Mara taught us some folk dances, and we often joined hands in a circle to practice them. We also had a couple of rock albums; we jumped around to the same songs every Friday night, singing along, and never tired of them. Theo used to purse his thick lips and dance around, shoulders moving up and down, imitating the lead singer. Everyone was amused, I most of all. The Europeans taught us Americans some of the steps to the contact dancing which was appropriate for many of the slightly slower songs. This type of dancing must have been popular in our home towns before we reached our teens; we had never learned it.

Theo and I spent much of that time with each other; we were establishing an intimate and deepening relationship. We always held each other for the slow dances, the mutual attraction growing.

Our group grew closer, too, in dancing and talking; those Shabbat evenings gave us further opportunity to learn about each others' homes and hopes. Jovial Dan was almost always accompanied by tall, thin Stan: a visually amusing pair. They were funny, and friendly with everyone. Even small, bespectacled Henry, also from our

American group, who generally gave the impression of cringing from the world, would be at our Moadon every week. Sometimes he even danced.

Friendships were nurtured, romances flourished, and we asserted our position and unity as a subgroup within a larger and increasingly welcoming community.

<u>The Solitude—I</u>

The social situation on the kibbutz was such that someone in my position rarely had a solitary moment. Even letter-writing and reading—quiet, personal pastimes—were generally done in the company of others. In the years before my time in Israel, I had spent many hours alone, studying, playing my flute, reading books. Overall, I found the living situation at the kibbutz to be pleasant, often enlivening, and so not frustrating, despite the almost constant company. But once in a while, I felt the need for freedom from the presence of others, for uninhibited solitude.

One spring afternoon, I went for a walk, alone. The weather was cool and the sky clear, except for a few wispy clouds. I left the Ulpan and strolled past other living areas to the edge of the fields, then down a tractor road between two different crops, between different shades of green. That led me to a row of dense pines, interrupted by the dirt road, which separated the fields from the orchards on my right and from barren land on my left. I crossed this line, then followed the string of cypress trees which edged the fruit trees. I was warming up and taking longer strides, the extra shirt I had been wearing now tied around my waist.

After I'd walked another ten minutes, the cypress trees took a sharp right turn, marking the end of the orchards. Ahead, on either side, lay only dusty earth; nothing grew. I paused at this point, on an upward slope of one of the low, broad hills which formed the land in that part of the country. Turning to view the many white buildings which lay behind me—easily noting the largest structure, the dining hall, up on the hill beyond them—I decided to go on, soon rounding the top of the small rise and starting down the other side. At this point, I experienced the strange sensation of no longer having the kibbutz or anything green in sight, no matter which way I turned. The sky was graying and the wind was picking up a bit. I assured myself that security lay not far behind me, and continued walking.

When I reached the top of the next dusty hill about ten minutes later, I noticed a short row of cypress trees a couple of hundred yards away. They looked like candle flames, broad and curved at the bottom, thinning, then pointed at the top. But they were cold—flames frozen, stilled—and very dark. I approached with curiosity, surprised that there was a cultivated area this far from the rest. Once close enough to see between the trees, I understood and stopped, staring at the small gray blocks that marked the graves, at the tan stones and small dark evergreen bushes which decorated the solemn site, and at the cypress trees which stood like sentinels on all four sides of the kibbutz cemetery. Trying to slow my breathing, I stood very still, having no desire to get close enough to read the inscriptions or walk between the tombstones. I was amazed at having discovered this hidden spot for which I had not been searching, and surprised at never having had the thought cross my mind that such a place must exist.

Gray clouds covered the early evening sky, and the wind had strengthened. Looking around in every direction, I found nothing to focus on but the graveyard. I felt chilled and hastened back toward the road. My heart raced as I ran over the bare hills. My pace slackened only slightly upon reaching the orchards, and a bit more once I was within the pine trees' boundary of the fields. Breathing deeply and steadily, I slowed to a strong walk once over the last hill, with the living area in sight.

The calming rhythm of my stride for the rest of the way back allowed me to realize the guilt I was feeling at having intruded. I would later tell Theo where I had been; I would not be anxious to blurt it out over dinner. My overwhelming emotion, however, was relief to be within sensation of other life, not alone in empty, unfamiliar surroundings—a solitary breath in the midst of barren land and unknown dead.

<u>The Bond—The Approach</u>

By this time, Theo and I had spent many hours alone together, talking, laughing, occasionally kissing, and relating stories of our pasts. We often talked for an hour or so at night, outside in the dark, before retiring to our respective rooms. Our sexual interaction was limited partly by circumstance, though I knew other volunteers were having sex. They either asked their roommates to sleep elsewhere, or decided not to mind the lack of privacy. I never considered imposing on quiet, shy Jen, and Theo had two roommates who would have been put out. Lack of privacy was not an option, as far as either of us was concerned. Our physical intimacy progressed slowly also due to my hesitancy. His experience was more extensive than mine, though we had had only one important relationship each in our youthful pasts. (I was eighteen; he was twenty). These were solemnly explained to each other, and mutual curiosity was satisfied.

We did have one night alone, in early March, when we took a two-day trip to Jerusalem. Volunteers were allowed one vacation day each month, to be used whenever we chose. Rather than the usual day-trip, Theo and I decided to go on Shabbat, spend the money to sleep there, and return Sunday evening.

We hitch-hiked to the city to save bus fare. Hitching was a safe and common form of transportation for young people in Israel; I also felt secure traveling with a man rather than another woman. So I hesitated only briefly when a big old truck, carrying two Arab men in traditional dress, stopped to pick us up. Theo and I climbed up into the cab with them, looking excitedly at each other. The Arabs talked happily and asked questions, but it was all incomprehensible to us. They spoke neither English nor Hebrew—we did not attempt Dutch—and neither Theo nor I spoke Arabic. Somehow, they gathered that we wanted to go to Jerusalem. It seemed they were heading there themselves. With some verbal sounds and many smiles and motions, they offered us tea from a large ornate thermos of some sort, and we accepted. As Theo passed me the cup, we again made eye contact equivalent to a reassuring squeeze of the hand.

By the time we reached Jerusalem, the Arabs apparently understood that I was from America, Theo from Holland, and that we both worked on a kibbutz somewhere near Beer Sheva (B-air Shev-ah). In their zealous hospitality, they practically dragged us with them to the Old City, where they would join their friends. It seemed difficult and ungrateful to refuse, so we allowed ourselves to be led to a small group of traditionally clad Arab men who sat at a little table on the sidewalk of a narrow street in the Arab quarter of the Old City. We were welcomed, seated, and offered small cups of strong and aromatic coffee. I, who had never liked coffee, found the exotic flavor delicious. I hoped our hosts would not be offended at my failure to consume the quarter-inch of pungent mud at the bottom of my cup. Since we really could not converse, we were allowed to leave after offering many thanks, in English and in Hebrew, to our driver and our hosts.

My eyes had opened wide to take in, for the first time, these scenes of white-robed men seated in groups outdoors, drinking coffee, smoking hashish from their large hookahs, and playing backgammon. The women were not to be seen sharing such leisure. We saw them later, as well as the barefoot children, as we walked by the markets and houses.

The Bond—The Setting

After roaming the Old City for a few hours, we decided to find a place to spend the night. We approached an old hotel just outside the Damascus Gate, by the Arab quarter, and entered. Like the rest of the city, the building was of tan Jerusalem stone. It had aqua-colored wooden shutters and doors, characteristic of the Arab style, and was darkened and worn. It looked charming to us, as well as inexpensive. Theo told the man at the desk that we wanted to sleep there. After showing our passports and paying for one night, we were pointed up a flight of stairs and given a key which opened the aqua door to a narrow room on the second floor.

Along the left wall were two single beds. Along the right wall were two small wooden dressers. Directly ahead in the far wall, almost touched by the end of the second bed, was a window which exposed a view of the Golden Dome in the Old City—a holy Muslim site, and a landmark of Jerusalem. We stepped inside and closed the door, studying the room which was easily encompassed in a glance. We did not look at each other, embarrassed at the situation which we had neither planned nor avoided.

To break the discomfort, I tossed my bag down on the closer bed and jumped onto it, landing on my knees and bouncing a couple of times. I said I was happy to be staying so close to the Old City, and that we were lucky to have such a view. Theo put his small pack on the other bed, a few steps away, and agreed. He sat down by the pack, perfectly still, and stared out the window. I looked at his back, at his broad shoulders down to which his fine blond strands reached, at his long thin arms resting on his bent knees, then past him, at the sky.

Inevitably, silence covered us. It stayed with us a while then gradually withdrew, and we managed to agree to go find some dinner. We took our money and passports and locked the door, leaving the uneasiness inside.

The Bond—The Meander

That evening, we wandered down narrow paths in the Arab quarter, between old stone walls lined with eager merchants and their colorful clothes. The prices, written in black marker on white paper tacked to little wooden posts which stood among the piles of shirts, were at least double what the merchants expected to get. Theo and I realized this as we observed others bargaining and buying. We had also heard from other volunteers that it was traditional and actually expected that the purchaser argue over the value of an item to be sold.

Buying a loose cotton shirt with swirls of decorative embroidery, I had my first experience haggling with an Arab salesman. The asking price was forty pounds (about ten dollars); I soon talked the merchant down to twenty. As I further lowered my offer, he became more argumentative. He was emphatic about that type of shirt being worth no less than thirteen pounds. I told him I had a friend who had bought one for less. He assured me that it could not have been the same type of shirt. I insisted that it was. He refused to lower the price. I said I would not pay that much for it and started to walk away.

There is nothing so convincing as naive self-assurance. I did not know then that walking away is one of the best techniques to use in such a bargaining situation. A bartering salesman will almost always take less than he wants, rather than lose the sale.

I was honestly planning to go without the shirt; he quickly called me back. We agreed on eleven-and-a-half pounds. (When I brought

49

the shirt back to the kibbutz, I found that it was indeed more extensively embroidered than the one I had believed was comparable.)

On other streets, Theo and I saw rows of large, beautifully crafted hookahs for sale, with inlaid glass of different colors. Many stood two feet high and had several hoses curving down and around their bases. They were like strange, magical creatures, especially to one who came from a country where marijuana was illegal, was smoked mainly by the rebelling young, and was disapproved of by most adults.

For dinner, we ate sandwiches of roast lamb in pita bread, a very popular food. The lamb was prepared by skewering thick slabs of meat onto a vertical rod about two-and-a-half feet high, then rotating the skewer as it cooked over a flame. The Arab vendor would use a sharp knife to make a stroke from top to bottom of the slowly turning cylinder of meat, allowing many small pieces to fall to the metal base and sizzle there momentarily. He then scooped them up and tucked them into a pocket of round bread; sometimes they were placed onto a piece of flat bread and rolled up. The meat was hot and spicy, the bread cool and fairly bland. Wandering and eating, relishing both, we eventually arrived back at the Damascus Gate. Passing through it, we exited the Old City.

The Bond—The Essence

Our hotel was just across the busy street and around the corner. At the sight of the aqua shingles, my stomach tightened in apprehension. We walked in and glanced at the man behind the desk, whose dark eyes followed us up the stairs.

Theo took the key from his pocket and opened the door to our room. As he closed it, I put my new shirt down on the dresser across from my bed. We discussed the Arab quarter, both realizing that our proximity that night had yet to be resolved. Despite that, we were relaxed and talkative, thanks to our experiences in Jerusalem so far. We peered out the window, which afforded little view, since it was dark by then. Stepping back from the window, we faced each other.

He put his hands around my waist and bent forward slightly. I leaned into the kiss and raised my arms to rest my hands on the back of his neck. We stood there kissing, for a while. The scene was familiar but thrillingly different from sitting together in the dark by the Ulpan. It seemed we were children with the freedom of adults. There was a night ahead in our own room, in a city new to us, in an ancient foreign land. So we allowed ourselves to be slowly swept by the combination of sensations, with great care for each other and some hesitancy.

We moved both packs to the bed by the window, turned the light off, and undressed down to our underwear. After a brief kiss, we turned back the covers of the other bed, and climbed in. We finished undressing, excited but cautious. We held, touched, kissed, and stroked each other's bodies for an hour or so, our first tentative mutual exploration. We did not have intercourse that night. Oddly, perhaps, that is something that was never to happen in the time our relationship lasted, though heated and satisfying sexual encounters did occur. Exhausted by the day, soothed by our naked warmth and intimacy, we finally fell asleep.

I later remembered, with a sense of wonder, how comfortable we were, lying there in the narrow bed. I recall a moment when we lay facing each other, our noses inches apart, one of my full breasts cupped in one of his long hands. Our eyes had adapted to the dim light filtering through the window; we were looking at each other and smiling.

The next morning we smiled again to see each other so close. After a bit of kissing and nuzzling, we agreed to get up and take advantage of our limited time in Jerusalem. As he pulled on his pants, Theo said,

"It's strange. In spite of last night, I still feel embarrassed getting dressed in front of you." I gave a small laugh, thinking it funny that anyone should feel comfortable saying such a thing. Yet it was reassuring, as I had the same sensation.

The Bond—The Homeland

We left the hotel, small packs on our backs, and headed for the Jewish Quarter of the Old City. That day, we shared our first view and experience of the Wailing Wall, the only portion of the old Hebrew Temple of Jerusalem remaining above ground. It was, somehow, an awesome sight: this huge, ancient tan stone wall, which people waited in line to approach. Many, many walked up very close to it, touched its old stones, ran their fingers over its rough cracks, and examined with fascination the millions of bits of white folded paper carrying written prayers, which were tucked into the myriad nooks and crannies the old wall offered.

We waited our turn, then approached. I felt that my heritage was contained in this monument I faced. Raising my hand to touch the wall, I lowered my eyes in recognition of its strength. Despite all the pictures I had seen, despite the fact that I knew it even from a distance, I was emotionally struck by the reality of standing before this overwhelming presence which seemed to have a life of its own, given it by the solemn faces and scribbled wishes offered to it in hope and prayer.

We followed a group of people to a small tunnel by the right side of the Wall. A guide inside showed us an excavation under way, allowing us to look deep into the ground along the back side of the Wall, down through the ages, to possibly one hundred feet more of wall built of the same stone. These stones formed the previously exposed wall, then were buried slowly by centuries of dust, until now they supported the worshiped Wailing Wall. Gazing down at the sepia tones, one could not avoid the crushing sense of being a momentary wisp of existence in time.

Theo and I left, impressed by both levels of the Wall we had seen. I was elated and could not be sure which view had been the more stunning.

We saw other fascinating sights in the Jewish Quarter that day, including beautiful Marc Chagall windows. By mid-afternoon, though, it was time to head back to the old hotel in the Arab Quarter.

After climbing the stairs and entering through the aqua door, we collected out few remaining belongings. Theo and I zipped our packs, surveyed the room, and embraced with a smile followed by one prolonged, delicious kiss. Then we went downstairs to return the key to the man with the dark, watchful eyes.

The Bond—The Return

We rode the bus from the Jerusalem station back to the kibbutz, occasionally mentioning things we had seen in the Old City. But for most of the trip, we looked quietly out the window. It was almost dark by the time we saw the familiar pattern of white lights across dim land which meant we were approaching the kibbutz. Theo and I glanced at each other, to indicate we knew our stop was next.

We had taken day trips with others before, and would take more by ourselves. Many days exposed us to unexpected views and experiences, all ending with a bus ride back to the kibbutz and that same pattern of lights. Traveling with the group, we would be discussing new information we had gathered, new sights we had seen. Once, returning from the beach with only Theo, we were tired and light-hearted, though his chest was badly sunburned. Relaxed by the desert sun's heat, not realizing its power, he had fallen asleep as we lay on our backs in bathing suits, one hand resting on his pale chest. When Theo awoke, he dropped his arm, sat up, then noticed the shape of his hand—in white—on his otherwise bright red chest. We laughed and hastened to cover ourselves. Later that evening, he proudly lifted his shirt to amuse the other volunteers with his unusual burn. Each time we returned to the kibbutz, we were happy and excited, like children after a field trip or a day at camp.

After our weekend in Jerusalem, we were happy but serious. This return was different. As we descended from the bus and entered the

E. R. Rubinstein

gate held open by the guard, we made the transition from a strange new dimension to the one we knew as everyday life. It was with a sense of fresh warmth and future closeness that we walked together to the Ulpan, hugged and kissed goodnight, and went to our separate rooms.

<u>The Maturing</u>

Due to my past Hebrew school training in the States, I was able to speak the language fairly well. Although I had stopped that portion of my formal education years earlier, my modest command of Hebrew far exceeded that of my fellow volunteers. (The Ulpan focused on teaching common terms and simple sentences). Because of this, I was asked to work in one of the children's houses, for two hours most afternoons.

This house had sixteen boys and girls, aged eleven to twelve, including the older of my kibbutz sisters. My responsibilities were to sort and fold their clean laundry, which was delivered to the house each day before my arrival, and to prepare open-faced sandwiches for their afternoon snack.

I arrived every day after their last class had ended, and stayed until they left to join their parents for a late afternoon visit prior to dinner. The children were never left for more than a few minutes at a time without an adult in the immediate vicinity. My duties were light for the time span available; my presence as a babysitter was the larger portion of the job.

After greeting the children, who welcomed me by surrounding me, I talked with them for a while. We would discuss my work, if they were interested, and their activities, and sometimes I would answer questions they had about the other volunteers. After that, I prepared their snack. This was their playtime; most of the next two hours was spent outside. They would occasionally come in to take a sandwich or get a book or a ball, and sometimes a few of them would keep me company as I cleaned up in the kitchen or sorted their clothes.

Although my Hebrew was fine for basic conversation, my vocabulary was not large. The children often became impatient with me when I would interrupt a question or comment to ask what some word meant. Still, they came to know me, and I to interact more easily with them. That time was usually enjoyable, as I was fond of them and felt privileged to have been assigned such a pleasant and relatively easy job in place of two more hours of picking fruit under the hot sun.

At the end of playtime, the children came in to change their clothes and get ready to go to their parents' apartments. Sometimes they had to be reminded and urged, sometimes scraped knees had to be cleaned or arguments broken up, but generally there was a smooth flow of activities. I left when they did, to go back to the Ulpan and wash up before dinner.

Occasionally, if his work were finished early, Theo visited me at the children's house. While I folded laundry, he would talk with me and joke with the children. They all knew him to be my boyfriend, and I sometimes saw them watching us with curiosity as we conversed for a minute or two, apart from them.

One day, after he had left, a couple of giggling girls came up to me. The taller one asked me a question. I had to ask her to repeat it, as it contained a Hebrew word I had not understood. She repeated it

58

emphatically, pursing her lips. At the sound of her elevated voice, a few other children came over, looking up at me expectantly. My kibbutz sister was there and managed to translate for me, through her laughter. The word was "kiss". The question had been, "How do you (plural) kiss?" It was funny because Theo, at six feet four inches, was a foot taller than I. They smirked and awaited a response. I shrugged my shoulders and smiled at them, making some feeble comment about his bending over. When I told Theo about it later, he laughingly asked,

"Did you tell them we lie down?" Of course, I would never have said such a thing to them, recognizing their innocence. Being charged with house responsibility each afternoon, I was a substitute parent, as were the "house mothers" who cared for the other members' children.

Another day, when Theo came to visit me, we had an argument. The topic was trivial; the anger erupted. I became cold and logical. He grew hot and loud. Although we stood a small distance from the play area, we were within sight and easy hearing of the children (as per my responsibilities). They noticed the commotion. Though both of us were emotional, he had less control. In response to some comment of mine, he slapped my arm, not forcefully, but rudely. I stifled the tears and told him he should never have done such a thing, especially in front of the children. My pain and anger were biting deep, but I was overwhelmed by a sense of shame and guilt that my charges had witnessed this. Amid the barrage of emotions, I realized at that moment, at the age of eighteen, that I was an adult. I was responsible for them first; Theo and I would have to handle our differences later. There was no point in attempting to converse further at that unstable moment. He left, and I went back to face the children.

They asked me—as I had known they would—why he had hit me. I took a deep breath, still trying to calm myself, and told them that I had said something which made him angry. They were indignant, sympathetic to my side, and insisted that he should not have hit me anyway. I agreed. They paused, not knowing how to assert their point more strongly, then one of them said,

"Tell him you won't be his friend anymore." The others indicated their approval of this solution.

It took all my self-control to avoid bursting into tears. I was deeply touched by their rallying to my cause, and realized how distant I was from their state of innocence. Though still quite upset over Theo's treatment of me, I knew he had been driven to frustration, for which I had been partly responsible. I was overwhelmed by the complexity of this minor ordeal. Meanwhile, the children looked up at me, awaiting my wisdom. This could be demonstrated, in their eyes, only by immediate agreement with their advice. Looking back at them, I responded,

"Well, maybe I won't be." After tolerating a few more insistent remarks, I managed to get them to shower and change their clothes.

They were distracted, but I was not. I felt tortured by the struggle between stubborn self-respect and forgiveness, between my desire to explain the situation to my friends, the children, and my comprehension of the hopelessness of such an attempt, between my craving for their devoted sympathy and the necessity of not breaking down in front of them, between the flood of emotions pouring forth from the child I was and the rational, heart-breaking control making an effort to exert itself through the woman I had become.

The Staple—Preparation for Consumption

We were surrounded by chickens in many forms. There were eggs available every day at breakfast, both hard and soft-boiled, there was often chicken at dinner, and of course there was chicken soup, while chicken stock was used to make other soups. This meant that kitchen work frequently involved the preparation of chicken, the details of which I learned during my weeks in that service.

The chickens eaten by us in the dining hall were fresh-killed. By the time they reached the kitchen, their heads and feet had been chopped off, they had been drained of blood, and the bulk of their feathers had been removed. It was up to us to extract the few remaining feathers and the many remaining quills. The latter was done by gripping a small, sharp knife, placing a quill firmly between the thumb and the blade, and pulling quickly upward. After all the quills had been removed in this way, the organs had to be pulled out. This was done by plunging one's hand into a slit cut in the bottom, grabbing the slithery insides, and dragging them out.

I had seen my mother clean chickens when I was younger. Though I had thought it rather disgusting because of the wet slipperiness of everything, it hadn't otherwise bothered me much. As a child, I had eaten chicken livers and chewed on their hearts, had seen the necks used in making soup. And I had certainly chomped on my share of drumsticks. But having to put my own hand inside a dead chicken and pull the organs out was a different experience.

Other people were doing it. I did it because it was my job, but my stomach churned.

I recalled the night that I, a five-year-old sitting at the dinner table with a chicken leg on the plate in front of me, asked my parents why we called this food we ate "chicken". I didn't understand it, since the big white birds which waddled around were also called "chickens". It was explained to me that these were pieces of those birds that we were eating; the drumsticks were their legs, the breasts their chests. I took it all in, found it harsh and cruel, realized that everyone did it and that I was used to it, and went on eating my dinner.

Working in the kibbutz kitchen, pulling guts from piles of chicken bodies and soaking them to remove any blood remaining in the veins, came close to making me ill. After a few days, I managed to trade the organ-pulling job for feather- and quill-pulling, with my French friend Christine. She found the former physically easier, as indeed it was, and not very disturbing.

After a rinse and cutting the chickens into pieces, the rest of the preparation was left to the chef.

E. R. Rubinstein

The Staple—Preparation for Market

We became intimately acquainted with another aspect of the chicken business when it was time for the adult chickens to be trucked to market. The "lool", or area in which the chickens were kept, consisted of two long rows of chicken coops. The floors of the coops were cement, so that they could be hosed down and thoroughly cleaned with a chlorine solution. This was done to avoid any contamination from the group of adult chickens being shipped out, to the next batch of new baby chicks.

The volunteers were called upon to help collect the chickens so that they could be boxed and loaded onto a truck. When I found I'd been assigned to work in the chicken houses, I asked a French volunteer named Henri (On-ree′) about the job which had come to be referred to as "chicken-chasing". He had been at the kibbutz for about two years, working almost exclusively with the chickens. He knew everything that went on there. Henri told me we'd have to try to catch them, that they would run away, but that we'd be able to overtake them or corner them. It was tiring work, he said, but it lasted only two days. By the end of the second day, we would have the coops emptied. It didn't sound like fun. When I got there, I found out how little fun it really was. Some people found it amusing, and I suppose it was, in a perverse way.

The coops were full of mature white chickens. They sent four of us in to catch them. The trick was to reach down and grab one by the legs, then hold it upside down in one hand while grabbing another with the other hand. I was taught to pass this second one, upside down, to the first hand, to join the first squawking chicken. The legs, just above the feet, are very thin, so grasping them with one hand, even a small hand like mine, was easy. Two more chickens had to be caught and added to the left hand—assuming you were right-handed, as I was—before it was considered full.

The harder part came next, when four more chickens had to be caught and held with the right hand. My left arm had to remain extended, as my left hand still held four chickens. The first two were not too difficult to catch with my right hand, but opening a few fingers to catch more, without releasing the ones already held, was tricky. It often took several tries to grab and hold a third and fourth.

The next step was to dodge the other sprinting volunteers and scrambling chickens and get to the doorway. At this point stood a kibbutznik who took all eight upside-down chickens at once, transferred by the feet from my hands to his. He stuffed them into a wooden crate, which was held out by another kibbutznik who was standing on a truck. The person on the truck would then close the lid and add that box to the stacks and rows already there. The chickens would right themselves once they were in the crate. Between the slats of the boxes we could see them moving around, though there was very little room for movement. Their constant squawking was background for our work all day long.

The process continued until the coop was empty. Earlier in the day, it was easier to catch them, since the population was so dense. As

65

it thinned out, the chickens ran faster. We were then forced to run farther and faster ourselves, in order to catch them. After the last box was closed and loaded, the truck drove away.

Sweaty and dusty, with tired legs and sore hands, we made our way back to the Ulpan.

The Staple—Preparation for the New Batch

The next job began after all the chickens had been packed off to market. The bulk of the dried-out solid chicken waste had to be shoveled up and dumped into canvas sacks before the floors of the coops could be swept clean and then hosed down with a disinfecting solution.

Mary, a Canadian volunteer who had arrived several months before we had, was in charge of assigning jobs to the volunteers. Reuben told her how many workers were needed for which areas, and she made up the list of job responsibilities. Henri, due to his valued experience and his preference, worked solely with the chickens; Theo had a regular job in the dairy. Betty was the first of our American group to establish a place for herself. She worked more and more in the dairy and became a regular there, trained to lead and milk the cows. I was one of the masses, shuffled around as needed. (My job at the children's house offered a break from that, for two of the six working hours).

Each evening, Mary informed us of the next day's assignments.

"OK, everyone," she announced that night. "Come see who'll be shoveling chicken shit tomorrow!" We groaned. The list included all but those who had regular jobs. Mary's name was not listed, either.

The next day, I walked into one of the coops and looked around for the waste we were supposed to clean up. I couldn't figure out where it was. Frank, another American volunteer, had to tell me that we were standing almost ankle-deep in it. The entire floor of each coop was covered with several inches of a powdery, pale gray, sand-like substance. I had thought it was some sort of soil or ash put down for the chickens to run around in. I was shocked at both the situation and the amount of work to be done.

We were each given a shovel, to be used to fill the nearest three-foot-high canvas sack, which hung on a metal frame. Once full, the sack was tied closed and removed by a kibbutznik, then replaced with an empty one. The work was hard on the back and rough on the hands. I coughed a bit during the morning of that first day, and more frequently later on. The fine dust was everywhere; it had a somewhat sweet odor which I soon found nauseating. I gagged on it, swallowed, and looked around. I saw the bent backs of other volunteers. Many of us worked with kerchiefs tied around our mouths and noses, but the dust still permeated. That afternoon, I blew my nose profusely and showered as soon as possible. I hesitated to complain, as others had the same nasty job to do. I had coughed so much, though, and had felt the mucous rise in my throat so often that day, that I decided to discuss it with Mary. I found her that evening, at the Ulpan.

"Hi, Mary. I was wondering if I could be assigned to a different job tomorrow," I said. "I was coughing a lot today from the dust, and I had a ton of phlegm in my throat. I really didn't feel well."

"Well," she responded, "I know it's a lousy job; nobody likes it." She was much taller than I, and (in my opinion) a bit haughty. I was not surprised at her lack of concern. "The list is already made up, though, and they need a lot of volunteers," she continued, peering down at me. "It should take only one more day. I'm sure you'll be all right."

That was all the time she would spend dealing with my problem. Mary had other job responsibilities, usually assigning herself to work in the pardess, and did not shovel with us. I had always felt she looked down on me; I was younger, and not too socially confident. In general, she spoke to me only when necessary and never with a smile. I saw her socialize with others happily and enthusiastically. She was quite friendly to Theo and a few of the other volunteers who were older and had been there longer.

In any case, I had my job assignment and reported bravely to work the next morning. After only an hour or so of shoveling, I was coughing so hard that I told the kibbutznik in charge how badly I was feeling. I could hardly breathe for more than a few seconds without going into a fit of coughing. My lungs were suffering; the phlegm kept forming in my throat. I was allowed to leave and told to do some other work for the rest of the day.

The nauseating sweet smell remained in my nostrils, the dust in my chest, as I walked haltingly back to the Ulpan. Theo happened to be on an errand from the refet at that time, and encountered me. He asked what had happened and supported me by the arm, as I frequently stopped to cough deeply or attempt to retch. He stayed with me while I got fresh clothes, and accompanied me to the washroom. I said I would be alright and, after some hesitation, he agreed to go back to work. I cleaned my face and neck, rinsed my mouth, and inhaled deeply, trying to clear my body of the whole unpleasant business.

The Feast

One late summer afternoon, several of the volunteers decided to organize a chicken barbeque, to be held at the Ulpan. We would gather there to build a fire in the pit at the center of the living area, prepare the meal, and cook it on the large grill. We would eat our supper outside that night, rather than going to the dining hall.

All those we asked were enthusiastic about the plan, so we discussed it with Henri. A tall, wiry Basque, he had thick, untamed brown hair, a beard to match, and dark, deep-set eyes. Though quiet and unable to speak English, Henri was quite friendly. He was proud of his job with the chickens, as it was a position of high responsibility. He worked there all year, driving a tractor, helping with the feeding, and having a say in the running of the coops.

It would take a day to make the preparations, Henri informed us. These involved his obtaining the required chickens and tools. By this time, he was second in charge of the "lool" (coops), so he had the authority, as well as the permission of the kibbutznik who was the head of the coops, to take the ten chickens we would need.

The following afternoon, we gathered around the Ulpan as Henri drove a small tractor up the dirt hill to the corner of our living area by the outdoor sink. On the small wooden platform he was towing were a few crates containing chickens. He unloaded the crates and opened one, taking a chicken out and closing the lid. Using an old tree stump as a chopping block, and lifting the hatchet he had brought, Henri held the squawking chicken down and quickly cut its head off. I watched in amazement as he tied it by its feet to a pipe above the large ceramic sink, and let the bright blood drain onto the white surface. He asked Frank to hand him the next chicken, and the process continued. It was fascinating and awful to me, especially my first view of the erratic movements of the proverbial "chicken without a head". I hung back with Betty and Christine, in a doorway of the adjacent building.

After the blood had been drained and the feet cut off—Henri quietly and efficiently taking care of the more distasteful bits of business—I ventured closer to help pluck the feathers. The striking event now became more commonplace, like working in the kitchen. Henri had disposed of the heads and feet, and the blood had been well rinsed down. The only remaining signs of slaughter were the chickens we were cleaning and cutting up.

By the time the parts were sizzling on the grill, there seemed little connection between them and the horror I had felt an hour earlier. When the meat was done, we ate.

The First Break

Reggie and I had begun to make music together most evenings, usually with flute and guitar, sometimes with two guitars. (I knew only a limited number of folk songs on the guitar and did not play that instrument nearly as well as I played flute). We improvised; we took turns choosing songs. Some evenings we had an audience, but often it was just us. All in all, we got along well and enjoyed both the music and each other's company.

A few weeks before the trip Theo and I took to Jerusalem, Reggie and I had been alone in their room, he playing guitar, I playing flute. At one point, we were taking a break, discussing what song should be next, when he moved a bit closer and slid his arm around my back. Holding me close for a moment, he leaned his hot cheek against mine. I remained fairly still, not responding to the embrace. When his lips brushed my cheek as he moved to kiss me, I turned away and hung my head. I felt badly offending this friend, if he did feel offended. I hoped he knew me enough to realize why.

"I'm sorry; I just can't," I said, having difficulty speaking at that moment. Reggie knew I liked him, and probably suspected I found him attractive—with his warm eyes, broad red cheeks, wavy brown hair, and trim build—as did several other female volunteers.

"Is there someone else?" he asked. I nodded, unable to make eye contact. "It's Theo, isn't it?" he guessed surely.

"Yes, it is," I responded, feeling clumsy and unkind. "I can't do this."

"I understand." Reggie nodded thoughtfully at the floor. "Well, um, maybe we ought to call it a night," he suggested.

"Sure, thanks," I said, facing him and trying to smile. I kissed his cheek then packed my flute away. We ended our music session a bit uncomfortably but as good friends, maybe better ones. I never mentioned it to Theo, and I doubt Reggie did either. There were still times to come when the three of us would happily spend hours together.

A couple of months later, in the warm spring, a friend of Reggie's in England contacted him at the kibbutz and invited him to join a rock group. Reggie was thrilled at the opportunity; he had been wanting to play guitar in a band. The day he told us that he would be leaving, I was shocked. I had become complacent, taking his companionship for granted. Reggie was dear to me; we had spent much enjoyable work and leisure time together. He was also a guitar-playing buddy, as well as a close friend of Theo's. Reggie was an integral part of the life I was enjoying as a volunteer at the kibbutz.

It took him about a week of planning: calling friends at home, booking a flight, and packing clothes. The day Reggie was to fly home, I said a tearful good-bye, then left him and Theo to their parting conversation. We would not accompany him to the airport. None of us had access to a kibbutz car, but Reggie was given a ride by a kibbutznik who was driving to Tel Aviv on business.

Theo found me back in my room at the Ulpan, visibly shaken. I recognized that the chances of either of us seeing Reggie again were very small. He had been a friend, but the extent of my unhappiness went beyond what he had meant to me. I was having great difficulty coming to terms with the loss of someone who had, to a large extent, helped define my existence of the preceding six months.

This disillusionment forced me to view my situation, and that of all my friends at the kibbutz, as not only temporary, but fleeting. I was afraid to see who would leave next; I felt uncertain about the next day and the day after. Most of all, I was terrified at the thought that Theo might go.

I had always associated him with Reggie. I had met them together, they had roomed together, and we had spent much time as a threesome. I sadly asked Theo if he was going to leave; he assured me that he would not. We talked about Reggie for a while, and I interrupted several times to ask that same question. Theo did his best to comfort me, always giving the same response.

<u>The Solitude—II</u>

My next venture beyond the usual paths of the kibbutz, but within its boundaries, occurred a month or so later, with Theo. That particular evening in late spring, we decided to go for a walk by ourselves, rather than joining the other volunteers after dinner.

The light was not yet fading as we took a path from the dining hall that led away from the living area, away from the refet and the lool, out toward the orchards. Beyond the dining hall behind us were no other buildings. It was the path I had followed the day I discovered the cemetery. When we reached the fork before the hill which shielded the view of the burial site, I led us in the opposite direction.

Paralleling the dark pines by the orchards, we continued, hand in hand, past the boundary of flame-like cypress separating the trees from the fields. We glanced at each other occasionally, but did not speak. The light dimmed, though the sun still glowed scarlet. Then, pausing along the dirt road, we witnessed a classic desert sunset; the huge glowing disc gradually slipped below the distant land.

Continuing in silence, we were surrounded by dusty hills and a sky whose color was only a paler version of the earth's. There were no longer any trees in sight, in any direction. We went on. The air itself seemed to take on a grayish tinge; the horizon became difficult to define. Evening had faded into dusk, then nothingness. We and the vanishing road seemed to follow. There was little security then, on a narrow path in the midst of empty desert land and fading light, far from home.

The effect on us of the solitude and obscurity was devastating. We slowed our pace. The hand I held seemed to belong to someone vague and foreign. There was nothing definite to lend assurance, no object or color or clarity or anything to grasp, except the hand which I did not know. The sensation estranged and frightened us both. Still in silence, observing each other's shadowy figures, we reacted.

Suddenly turning, we ran back in terror—not so much to find light and others, as to find ourselves.

The Home

In the middle of May, Franz and Thomas left the kibbutz. I had been able to communicate only slightly with Franz, due to my inability to speak German, but had enjoyed his company and our brief mutual language lessons. Theo was sorry to see Franz go, as they had become quite friendly. It had often amused me to see them standing together, like differently colored bookends. Both were very tall and broad-shouldered, though thin, with strong facial features and shoulder-length hair. Theo was green-eyed, blond, and fair; Franz had hair and eyes that were almost black, and a ruddy complexion.

Thomas was Swiss-German as well. He looked, to me, like a bright drawing from a child's book of fairy tales. Fairly short, with curly blond hair, a round face, and red cheeks, Thomas had a big smile for everyone. He was liked by all and was friendly, always, though he did not appear to have sought or formed any close bonds while at the kibbutz.

By the time of their departure, Henri and Ingrid were living together in one of the shacks that had housed the original kibbutzniks. Their pairing had struck me as odd, despite the clear mutual physical attraction. He was serious; she was capricious. Neither spoke the other's language, nor any other common language. Yet they were obviously quite in love, frequently hugging and smiling blissfully at each other.

Franz and Thomas had shared another such shack. Theo and I recalled that Henri had gotten a key the previous month, from departing volunteers, in order to have a private room for Ingrid and himself. We were tempted to do the same but knew we should discuss it with Reuben first. Franz gave Theo his key; Theo and I took it to Reuben and asked if we could have the vacant cabin. He grinned as he looked back at us, realizing our closeness over the preceding months, and agreed.

Flushed with excitement, we went back to the Ulpan to pack up our clothes and move. We told our roommates, who were happy for us. Jen, very serious and fairly quiet, never danced wildly and late in the Moadon on Shabbat, or spent much time talking in a room full of chatty volunteers. She played guitar very well and preferred to spend her free time either practicing, or talking with one person at a time. We got along nicely and talked quite a bit when we were in our room together. She might have been sadder to see me go but for her developing relationship with a Canadian named Terrence.

He was from British Columbia and had arrived alone at the kibbutz, shortly before our group. Mary—of the job list—and a friend named Lulu, traveling together from Vancouver, had been at the kibbutz for a couple of months by then. As they had much in common with Terrence, those three had immediately become friendly. It was not long before he and Lulu became romantically involved. When Lulu and Mary decided it was time to move on, I had the distinct impression that Terrence was disturbed. I was not fond of Mary and did not know Lulu very well. I was, however, looking

79

unsuccessfully for Lulu in order to say good-bye to her the day they were to leave. I thought she'd be in her room packing and was surprised that she was not around. When she finally turned up at the Ulpan, I wished her well then asked where she'd been.

"I was saying good-bye to Terrence," she answered, and laughed. I gathered she had thoroughly enjoyed her physical relations with him but thought nothing of leaving.

After that, Terrence, who was an excellent folk guitarist, began spending more and more time with Jen. They practiced together and often played duets. At meals, they always sat together. In quiet, reliable Jen from Montana, Terrence found a girlfriend with a personality opposite Lulu's. He was apparently quite happy. By the time I told Jen I was moving to a shack with Theo, she was immersed in her feelings for Terrence.

Carrying our bags, Theo and I left the Ulpan and walked across the road, then up a small hill to the shacks. Ours was the building with the skull of some long-dead animal, probably a sheep, hanging from a nail next to the door. We never knew who had mounted it there or why, but we left it. Opening the door to our new room, we noted the large window, two metal spring beds with thin but reasonably comfortable mattresses (as in the Ulpan rooms), two old wooden dressers and two small wooden night tables. Those of us who stayed in the shacks would walk to a small building about fifty yards away to reach a sink and three toilets.

Happily unpacking our clothes, we placed them in the dressers. We pushed the beds together and set a night table on either side.

When we had finished arranging the room, Theo and I looked each other over then moved together and embraced tightly for a long moment. As it was time to go to dinner, we kissed briefly then walked, hand in hand, to the dining hall.

<u>The Celebration</u>

On my nineteenth birthday, we lay in bed almost all day. It was Shabbat. We went to breakfast, then celebrated together in our little cabin. Theo presented me with a gift he had bought in Jerusalem—a large silver star of David on a silver chain. It was unusual, intentionally blackened in areas, having an appearance unlike the whitish, polished silver I was used to seeing. I put it on then, and wore only that.

It was one of several occasions on which intercourse was approached but not attained. Somehow not ready, I tensed as we began. Then it hurt, and we stopped. I never was quite sure why I seemed to have a psychological resistance; I doubted it was physical. Theo would not continue, at my indications of discomfort. We both believed that in time, it would happen.

Despite that impasse, the day was long and pleasurable. When we joined our companions in the dining hall that evening, they remarked upon my new necklace. No one asked where we had been.

The Departure

Frequent summer scenes with friends—resting under the tall pines which surrounded the kibbutz pool and taking turns diving or jumping off the board—were over. It had been fun to watch Mara show off her diving skill those afternoons, turning neat somersaults in the air before hitting the water. We were fortunate to be at a kibbutz which could afford the luxury of a pool, and we enjoyed it fully. But by late July, most of the volunteers we had known from our first weeks at the kibbutz were gone.

Henri had left for Greece two months earlier, with Ingrid, whose flirtatious charm had attracted and held him. She had found someone who would love and care for her in exchange for her devotion to him. They planned to travel around the Greek isles, camping on beaches, until their money ran out. Then they would find a way to make more money.

Most of my American companions had returned home before the third week in August, when our service was supposed to end. Betty, an exception, had fallen in love with a warm, handsome kibbutznik—the best relationship she'd ever had, she told me—and planned to remain indefinitely. Another from our group, friendly Dan, planned to leave in August, spend a month or so at home in New York, then return to the kibbutz permanently. Jen and Terrence had left for Canada in early July, hoping to make a living playing guitar together.

The rest of our friends, including Christine, had been gone for at least a month.

Watching them go, one by one, had less impact on me than Reggie's long-ago departure. Theo and I had learned to adjust, with lessening pain, to the absence of each. Despite the sting, we realized that there were other people and places in our friends' lives drawing them away. And eventually, we knew that it was time for us to go, too.

I had taken a leave of absence from college for the spring semester and was expected to attend in September. My parents were counting on my late summer return, and were anxious to know when I would fly back to New York. The thought of leaving Theo, though, was unbearable, and my open-ended airline ticket was good for three more months.

Having met Europeans who had told me of their countries, I was desperate to travel and explore more of the world. Theo wanted to go with me.

Would any harm be done, I wondered, by taking another semester off? My academic performance had been very good; I thought the university would readmit me the following January. I decided to write a letter explaining that my travel plans had been extended and that I would return for the spring rather than the fall semester.

My parents, however, were not as easily convinced of the reasonable nature of my extended leave. They were horrified at the thought of my traveling in unknown places with an unknown boyfriend. I wrote of my intentions; they called me at the kibbutz.

The debate was emotional and difficult; they used every argument in their power, including guilt inducement, to dissuade me.

But I held the plane ticket. It had been issued in my name, and it was up to me to reserve the return flight. My hand shook as I looked down at it; the opportunity was irresistible. I knew I had to go to Europe, though it meant defying my parents.

Theo and I discussed where we should travel. I wanted to see Paris; we wanted to go together to Holland. My ticket (already paid) entitled me to make one stop and continue on to New York from a different location, if I so chose, providing the second location was farther west. He could buy a less expensive ticket to a country further east than France or the Netherlands, then we could work our way west on land.

After much discussion, our plan was set and the reservations made. We would fly to Austria, hitchhike from there through Switzerland to France, and then through Belgium to the Netherlands. I would fly to New York from Amsterdam, in time to join my family for Thanksgiving.

Never having dreamed of such a venture on departing for Israel, I had arrived with two suitcases. Dan, however, had a large backpack which he did not need, except to bring his clothes home. In New York, he lived less than a half hour's drive from my parents. He offered to trade his pack for my larger suitcase; we would get together to exchange them when I returned to the States. I would pack unnecessary clothing in my smaller suitcase and send it to my parents' house. With that bit of logistics worked out, we were set.

Together, Theo and I visited each of our kibbutz families to say good-bye. I received a large picture book of Israel, as a gift, from mine. The touching inscription said it was to remind me of the days we had spent together. I promised my twelve-year-old kibbutz sister that I would write and also look forward to reading her letters.

On a hot August day, with packs on our backs and entreaties from the kibbutzniks to return soon, we left Israel.

<u>The Mountains—Austria</u>

We flew to Vienna and made our way, by train and on foot, to the youth hostel. Several days were spent roaming narrow old streets and studying stained glass church windows. Hitchhiking into Salzburg, we explored that city also. All sights and buildings were wonderful to me, as I had never seen anything like them before.

Our occasional conversations and dealings with store clerks as well as people we met in the youth hostel were simple, thanks to Theo's command of the German language. I felt relatively helpless. But I read signs carefully, asked Theo questions, and gradually built up a small vocabulary of common words and phrases.

We lived on bread, cheese, yogurt, and apples, always careful with expenditures. If our money ran out, the trip would be over. Occasionally, we took trains, but most of the distance we covered was due to the help of strangers who gave us rides for the sake of conversation, curiosity, or good will.

Theo and I were less than compatible on several occasions, as we began our tour. Perhaps it was due to the instability of being on the road; I suspected I was irritable also from a sense of such reliance on him for communication with the surrounding world. We argued on the street in strange cities, once separating for hours, finding each other again back at the hostel. An event in the mountains of Tyrol forced us closer.

We had arrived in a small town on a Sunday. No banks were open, and we had little Austrian currency left. Generally, we cashed our traveler's checks as needed and had no trouble; this time we had underestimated. In search of cheese and bread, we entered a grocery store high in the Alps. The bread we bought was always rich and satisfying, and the cheeses had flavors new to my tongue. We took a loaf of bread from the shelf and chose a wedge of cheese. We had barely the amount of money we needed, and thought of buying another piece of cheese and some apples if we'd had more.

A middle-aged couple entered the store while we were assessing our financial state. Their dress made us certain they were tourists, possibly American, and we decided to ask if they would be willing to accept a signed five or ten dollar traveler's check in exchange for some Austrian currency. We approached them with our request. They at first appeared suspicious then seemed to realize that we were honest; we hopefully awaited their response. Looking us up and down, they took in the backpacks, jeans and boots, my long loose brown hair, Theo's bangs, which almost reached his eyes, and his shoulder-length blond strands. They asked how much we needed. We told them that the equivalent of five American dollars would be enough, and I pulled a small packet of traveler's checks from my pack. The man handed Theo some Austrian cash then shook his head at me, as I took out a pen. He pointed to my neck, and said.

"That's enough for me." I glanced down and saw the large star of David that Theo had given me, hanging from its silver chain. Looking up in surprise, I met the eyes of this stranger who had been touched and generous. We thanked him, paid for our food, and left, still amazed.

As we walked the two miles to the town's youth hostel, Theo and I discussed the encounter. I thought the man must have been Jewish, but Theo did not agree that was necessarily the case. He told me that Hitler had been born in this region of Austria, a fact of which I had been unaware. Having grown up in a town where the majority were Jews, and after seven months in Israel, it had not occurred to me to be self-conscious about the silver star I wore. The incident awakened me to the largely Christian, potentially anti-Semitic realm I had entered.

Raised in a Dutch, non-religious Christian family, Theo had an awareness of our surroundings which I had not. I attributed it to his having grown up in Europe. His parents' generation had been much more affected, as a whole, by the second World War than were most Americans of the same age, despite the fact that many Americans had fought and died in that war. Europeans are surrounded by evidence of the war; they live with, and transmit to their children, a higher level of consciousness regarding those events than we learn. I felt that my innocence in wearing the star of David in the Tyrol had not been deserving of a reward. However, once I understood the extent of its meaning there, I determined to continue to wear it bravely.

We plodded along to the hostel, carrying our loads, in comradery and pensive silence.

The Mountains—Switzerland

The glorious snow-covered crown of western Europe was like a fairyland to me—the air so pure, the grass so green. We encountered brown mountain goats, soft and friendly, and the language was spoken with a lilt which I knew the Germans found offensive but which I found charming.

Aside from minor squabbles, Theo and I shared a few wonderful weeks in the Swiss cities and Alps. We walked together, until we were weary, through Zurich, Lucern, and Geneva, thrilled by the gorgeous lakes, the intricate architecture.

Our five-day stay at an Alpine hostel, reached only by cable-car or a half-hour walk from the nearest road, was truly an escape from the rest of the world. From there, misty mountains afforded us several spectacular hikes, including a pink sunset behind white clouds, superimposed on white snow-covered mountainsides. Standing ankle-deep in snow in my wet boots, I felt I was floating. Mesmerized by that view, we were willing to end the moment only because the sun would soon be gone.

In this cloud-enshrouded retreat, we met an American from Alabama, named Wade. He was traveling as we were, on a similar budget, and had bought a small old German auto in which to drive around Europe. Wade told us of the beauty of the French countryside but was more excited about the Swiss Alps. As we sat in the dining hall, Theo and I shared stories with him of our experiences in Israel and Austria. We enjoyed each others' company so much that we decided to travel together for a while. Leaving the hostel, we three took the cable car down the side of the mountain to the valley below, where Wade's car was parked.

We then headed to another Alpine town with a youth hostel, once stopping to explore one of the many glaciers in that region. Parking at the side of the road, we carefully climbed out. The rocky edge dropped precipitously, and through the mist we saw a mass of ice, not far from the road. We could barely make out the far edge of the frozen flow. Dark birds flew overhead, swooping close to the glacier then sweeping away, under a cold gray sky. The scene was impressive and intimidating, we tiny humans facing this huge creeping power. Our new-found friend was thrilled.

"Those birds sure know about glaciers," said Wade. "What a place this must be to live in!" We stared for a few more minutes, shivering, then glanced at each other to acknowledge the cold. With a last, long, awestruck look at the icy expanse, we returned to the small car and drove on, the highway hugging the steep mountain's edge.

At one point, we stopped to pick up two young Swiss men who were hitch-hiking. They crowded into the back seat with me, smiling and appreciative and chattering in Swiss German. Due to their accents, Theo was barely able to converse with them. It seemed they were from Zurich, on a week's vacation in the mountains, and were headed for a town along our planned route. I could not understand a word of theirs; neither could Wade. But their light-hearted mood was apparent, and we were happy to be with them for a while. As we drove through the mist, catching glimpses of masses of snow-covered rock, they pulled small wooden recorders from their pockets and played a duet of "You Are My Sunshine". We laughed as we tried to sing along, all of us recognizing the tune, none being sure of the words.

After dropping our merry passengers by the road at the specified point, Wade, Theo, and I continued into the next tiny town, where we would sleep. We shared dinner, which consisted of groceries purchased at the local store, then spent the night at the youth hostel. In the morning, we explored the narrow streets of the picturesque village, then roamed the nearby hills later in the day. After another night at the hostel, Theo and I said good-bye to our companion and set out for the farm of a Swiss friend from the kibbutz.

The Farm

Theo called Franz from a pay telephone in a nearby city. We had been invited to visit him at the farm where he lived and worked with his parents and brother, in case we were in Switzerland. This was based, I knew, on his relationship with Theo. Franz still spoke almost no English and I, practically no German. (We had not persevered in our joint language studies, although my Dutch had certainly improved). In addition to this, he was rather shy. I therefore felt somewhat uncomfortable accepting the invitation, though Theo was eager to go.

We hitched to a road near the farm, then walked the last few kilometers. Sweaty and tired, we finally arrived and were warmly welcomed by Franz, who was quite fond of Theo. His family offered handshakes and examining looks. They showed us to the room which would be ours in their comfortable, though not very large, farmhouse. The high bed was made with snow white sheets, a fluffy white down comforter, and the biggest pillows I had ever seen. These were covered in crisp white pillowcases. With relief, we set our packs down then followed Franz out of the house to see their land, on which they grew strawberries.

By the time we walked out to the field, Franz' father was back at his hoeing, a labor he had interrupted in order to greet us. We said hello, and I asked Theo to request the father's permission to take his picture. (My camera was with me always, throughout our trip).

Hearing "ja", I snapped the scene: this wiry middle-aged man, hoe in hand, in the midst of low green plants stretching to the right and left borders of the image, and far into the distance. I had learned enough German to understand Franz's father when he looked me in the eye and said "ein Schweitzer bauer" (a Swiss farmer). I was immediately ashamed; he was titling my photograph of him, imagining it in an album with that caption. It had not been my intention. I was not considering the fate of my pictures as I happily clicked away. I had already taken one of Franz and his mother and brother, standing in front of the house. I wanted a picture of his father, also. Feeling this man's experienced, sarcastic, though not unkind gaze, I looked down. He probably did not know I had understood; I could say nothing in German to explain myself. Theo broke the moment by asking some questions about the growing season and markets, then we returned to the house with Franz.

I felt helpless and grateful during our brief visit. After Theo explained that we had dirty clothes we needed to wash, Franz's mother filled the bathtub for us, with most of the hot water available at one time. We washed our jeans, our underwear, and a couple of shirts, then filled the tub again, with cold water for a rinse, and hung our clothes outside on the line to dry. Later, we were treated to a family country dinner, all seated around the large wooden table in the spacious kitchen. There was a huge pot of thick soup to start, followed by chicken (which was probably delicious but did not appeal to me), fresh cooked vegetables, and dense brown bread. Full and tired, we slept soundly amid the luxuriously deep feather pillows and comforter.

By the time we awoke and dressed the next morning, Franz's brother and father were at work in the field. Franz would have been, too, except he was waiting for Theo and me. His mother made us coffee and served us bread. She offered more food, but after the previous evening's meal, bread was enough. We begged her to go about her business without feeling obligated to do more for us.

Franz, Theo, and I sat at the big table and conversed; that is, they talked and I sipped my coffee, occasionally comprehending bits and pieces. Franz told us that he planned to visit Thomas, his former roommate from the kibbutz, the following weekend. He said he was sure we would be welcome also. It sounded like fun, so at Theo' request, Franz called Thomas. We should please visit as well; Thomas was happy to hear we were nearby. Due to the time it would take to hitch-hike, Theo and I decided to leave that day. Franz would meet us later, at the end of the workweek. We packed our clothes, which were almost dry, and, with many thanks, said good-bye to the family.

<u>The Reunion</u>

It took us two days to reach Thomas; we had difficulty getting rides on some of the smaller roads. A man who picked us up one evening went half an hour out of his way, to bring us to the door of the youth hostel where we planned to spend the night. Late the following day, after several rides and several kilometers of walking, we arrived in Thomas' village and found our way to his house.

There, we were shocked to be greeted by not only Thomas, but also by Henri and Ingrid. She was pregnant; it had happened in Greece after they ran out of contraceptives. They had decided to get married in Sweden, where Henri would work as a roof-sweeper—clearing the snow off houses—and Ingrid would raise their child. She glowed, and he radiated pride. They were still very much in love. On their way north, they had stopped to visit Thomas.

He and Henri were good friends, communicating in French. For Thomas, this was almost as easy as speaking German. For me, it was a relief and a delight to finally be able to participate in the conversation, thanks to my ability to speak French. And it was exciting for all of us to be together, this time in Switzerland.

I was glad to see Henri, and pleased at his happiness. I had never expected to see him and Ingrid again, once they left the kibbutz to wander the beaches of Greece. It was strange to find them, unexpectedly, in a place where I had never been, and to see them as a soon-to-be-married couple with plans for a family life together. I felt so young, so far from that.

Thomas was rosy-cheeked and bright-eyed, as usual. His father was a butcher, which I had not known, and apparently the business did very well. He eagerly showed us around the packing area, where all sorts of sausages were produced. Everything was white-tiled, gleaming and clean; we were spared any encounter with animals intended for food. They were brought there, Thomas explained, only to be butchered, and were not raised on their land.

His family's house was large and modern. We had a dinner consisting of more kinds of "wurst" than I ever knew existed, as well as many other dishes. We ate casually, filling our plates then sitting on chairs and couches in the modern living room. I enjoyed the food and my surroundings, still unable to get over my amazement at the group gathered there.

The next day we walked together around the countryside and into town, sharing our recent experiences. Late that afternoon, as we sat talking in the yard, Franz arrived. He greeted everyone with pleasure, sat down, and joined in the conversation. We all shared another generous and delicious supper. My body was satiated and my mind was happy among the familiar faces and personalities. For the first time since we had left the kibbutz, I felt quite comfortable, with a sense of being at home.

Theo and I spent one more night there. Despite the companionship and warmth of the reunion, we felt compelled to move on. There was still France to be seen, and then Holland, and it was already October. I was supposed to be home the third week of November.

With thanks and hugs and the exchange of addresses, we left our friends and walked down the small street, away from Thomas' house.

The Shock

From Switzerland, we hitch-hiked to Paris; it took three rides followed by a train into the city. I was very excited to be in that rich place about which I had read and heard so much.

In the youth hostel, which was easily found, Theo and I were each given a bed in a large room with other members of our sex. The place was crowded, with poor lighting and filthy toilets, and had a feel unlike that of any other hostel we had been in. We spent only the time it took to pay, drop our packs on our cots, and wash our hands and faces, before leaving to explore the city.

Walking around Paris was fascinating, as scenes from photographs came to life in a fresh dimension. I knew my way from the Arc de Triomphe to the Place Vendôme from a remembered map in my French language book. I thought I knew what the Eiffel Tower looked like, but was unprepared for its actual appearance—strikingly huge, and somehow romantic. Standing under the center, Theo and I stared up in awe at the size and construction of the arches and the amazing height of the tower. We strolled along the Seine, taking in the flowing gray water, the stone bridges, the portrait painters stationed every few meters who tried to get our attention and business, and the varied crowd of which we were a part.

We wanted to spend time at the Louvre but agreed to save that lengthy treat for the following day. Wandering through Paris for the first time was an experience to be enjoyed at leisure, to be savored.

We ate dinner at a small restaurant, where the modestly priced food was tasty and satisfying. As it had been a tiring day of traveling and walking, we slowly headed back to the hostel for the evening.

Shortly after entering, we realized that a large crowd was gathered in the common room. It took a moment to see this, as the light was so dim and the place mobbed. A television set hung from the ceiling; this was the first hostel in which we had seen one. Everybody seemed focused on it, so Theo and I squeezed our way in to get a view of the screen.

Israel had been attacked by Arabs. The details were unclear. It was Yom Kippur, a high holy day of prayer and fasting for Jews. An attack on Israel on such a day was almost unimaginable. The world was shocked and anxious.

I turned to stare at Theo and he looked solemnly back at me. We squeezed each others' hands, hardly able to believe this news. Throughout our time at the kibbutz, Israel had been so calm—and we'd left only two months earlier. We were frightened and struck by the changeability of life and security. Young kibbutzniks must be involved in the fighting, or preparing to go. Now we were far away, dependent upon impersonal televised reports for information which so strongly affected the people among whom we had lived and worked. We stood and watched, with the others, until it appeared there was no more to be learned at that time.

After the crowd dispersed, Theo and I discussed the situation and the soldiers we knew, guessing who might be called upon to participate.   We finally went to bed in our respective rooms, nervously wondering about the fate of our friends.

The Vineyards—the Plan

Our next visit was to Christine, the French woman who had been one of my best friends at the kibbutz. She lived in a rural area not far from Paris, where Monet had painted many of his famous flowering fields.

We did not get there by the end of the first day of hitch-hiking and spent that night at a small hostel in a tiny village along the way. Sometimes we got rides fairly easily, but had trouble during a rainstorm, which we waited out beneath a bridge.

It was the second week of October; we had told Christine to expect us in mid-autumn. The afternoon we called from a nearby town, she was at home. We followed her directions along the green and rolling terrain and had a pleasant half-hour's walk.

We were delighted to see each other again; Christine's mother seemed equally glad. Christine's father had died years earlier; the two women still lived in their brick house, with the addition of Christine's Israeli dog. After the puppy's mother, a large tan short-haired mutt, was run over on the road just outside the kibbutz gate, she had adopted him and later insisted on taking him back to France. The initial greeting over, they offered us a small spare bedroom upstairs. Theo and I left our packs there, washed our faces, changed our shirts, and went downstairs.

While Christine's mother cooked dinner, we babbled in French about our travels and our recent reunion at Thomas' house. We

102

shared our concern about the recent violence in Israel; Christine knew no more than we did. I was happy to be with her again, and interested to see her lovely native setting. The four of us shared a dinner of some sort of rich pâté baked in rolled dough, along with a tomato salad. Her mother was casual and friendly; she was curious and delighted to hear of our experiences. She also asked about our homes and families, and seemed pleased that we had come to visit her daughter.

The next morning, Theo, Christine, and I, accompanied by the dog Pilpel ("Pepper", in Hebrew, aptly named for his coloring) took a walk past fields of wildflowers to the town bakery. At the small stone building, we bought fresh baguettes—long, narrow loaves of crusty bread—and jam. We wandered back and ate without her mother, who had already left for work. Christine prepared bowls of coffee for us, with plenty of milk, which we lifted to our mouths with both hands. It was fun and apparently common practice, at least in the country. We ate the freshly baked baguettes with butter and jam. Everything was delicious, and we stuffed ourselves.

We had told Christine, while on the kibbutz, that we wanted to pick grapes in France. She now informed us that her brother, Joseph, had found a place to work and that we could go there also. Our pay would be by the day, and we would be given a room to sleep in, which cost would be subtracted from our wages. Theo and I were excited at the prospect and said we would go. We planned to leave that day, as she told us there was plenty of work, this being the height of the harvest season. She would join us the following day, after telling her mother of her plans and spending that night at home.

We hitch-hiked our way to the Loire valley. It should have taken only one day but took two, due to difficulty getting rides. At dusk of the first day, we were close to a small inn. We had waited patiently by the road, with thumbs out, for almost an hour, but no ride had been offered. Guessing at the cost of a room at the inn, we weighed it against the darkening sky and decided to spend the money. We walked down the hill to the inn and inquired, but the large female owner said she had no rooms. She eyed our long hair and backpacks suspiciously. It was getting late, we explained, and we were having trouble getting a ride. We asked if she knew of any other place we could stay. No, there were none, she claimed, and said we should walk farther up the road to try to get a ride. Finally, Theo and I did so, away from the village where we were sure we were not wanted.

As we waited patiently, higher up along the road, it grew dark. Eventually, we accepted the fact that we would not get a ride that night. We climbed a small wooden fence nearby, to sleep in a field. It was cold and damp by then, and the time spent standing still—as the air moistened and cooled—had chilled us even more. We curled up in our sleeping bags but could not generate enough heat to relax. After a half-hour of shivering, we resorted to putting one of our sleeping bags inside the other and squeezing in together, in order to maintain enough warmth to get some rest. It was ridiculously tight, but we managed to fall asleep.

Early in the morning, I felt something soft press against my head. Opening my eyes, I saw dew-covered grass and the edge of my damp sleeping bag. I raised my head a few inches and jumped slightly upon seeing the nostrils of a large brown horse which had gently nudged me in my sleep. Smiling, I reached out to stroke her nose, but she ambled away. My movement awakened Theo, who laughed when I pointed out the horse and told him what had happened. It was just as well, he said; we should get going before anyone saw us. So we inched out of the bags, rolled them up, and loaded them onto our packs. Walking the twenty meters to the road, we climbed back over the low fence, and started along our way.

A kilometer or so from that field, we got a ride. One more ride and several hours later, we found ourselves in the lush valley of the Loire River, surrounded by rolling hills covered with row after row of grape vines.

The Vineyards—the Labor

We followed Christine's brother's directions to the small family vineyard where we were expected, arriving late in the afternoon. The heavyset owner came out to meet us as we approached his large stone house. Once we had introduced ourselves, he relaxed. His name was Jean, he told us, and we were welcome. This was his business, along with his father, who was old but still did some work. We followed him to the yard beside the house, where we encountered Christine, dog at her side, and her brother. She immediately asked us, in mock outrage, what had taken so long; she had not expected to arrive before us. She complained that we should have been there the previous day. We explained our problematic trip, complete with an imitation of the snobby female innkeeper, but she continued to shake her head.

Jean then led us to his office, and asked how long we wanted to work. One week, we said. He told us that we would be paid by the day, but that we would not be paid until we left. He asked whether we needed a place to sleep; apparently, many people from the surrounding villages worked during the harvest and went home at night. We said we did want to stay there; he told us how much that would cost and what our pay would then be. We agreed, glad for the opportunity and the prospect of making any money at all to take away with us.

Next, he showed us to our room in a smaller stone building, about one hundred meters from the house. This he called the Annex; the only other person sleeping there would be Joseph, Christine's brother. She had a room in the main house, which was already filled to capacity with family and workers. We found our large stone room charming, though to many it would have been merely dark, rustic, and old. Joseph's room was nearby, though we rarely crossed paths. Theo and I left our packs and followed Jean back to the big kitchen in the main house.

It was evening by then, and time for supper. Famished after our long day, we eagerly anticipated the meal. About twenty people were there, beginning to seat themselves on the wooden benches on either side of a large wooden table. Christine was waiting for us; we sat down together. Joseph came over to chat briefly with us; we thanked him for making our arrangements. He had picked grapes at this same vineyard the previous year and knew some of the other workers; he sat at the other end of the table with them.

The supper was large, consisting of several courses, though I learned the next day that lunch was even bigger. Afterwards, we talked a bit more with Jean, telling him briefly about our backgrounds and recent travels. We spent another half hour or so with Christine, then left for the Annex.

At six the next morning, we were awakened by a clanging brass bell. Theo and I dressed hastily, as the room was chilly and damp. We then walked over to the house, where several pickers were already seated at the table. After greeting them, we also sat down. The others, male and female, were all congenial but did not seem particularly interested in us. I was glad, as I had not enjoyed the scrutiny of strangers to which we had occasionally been subjected over the previous month.

Jean's wife quickly placed bowls of steaming coffee before us. As was customary, we added copious amounts of milk from the large bottle. We also added a few of the small sugar cubes which were set out in bowls. Christine came in and joined us. We exchanged inquiries as to how well we'd slept, then drank our coffee.

Soon there were more people and louder chatter, then large bowls of boiled eggs and baskets of bread and pots of hot cereal were being passed around the table. There was plenty to eat and drink, but we wondered about the contents of the clear wine bottle filled with a clear fluid, which had a spigot shaped like a duck perched on top. We saw more than one person take a sugar cube and drip a small amount of this liquid onto it, then eat it. Theo and I asked Christine about this; she told us it was aquavit. As that meant nothing to us, she explained that it was a strong brandy, distilled from fermented grape skins. We were taken aback that people would consume this at breakfast, but of course, we had to try it ourselves. A drop alone on the tongue would burn, with almost no flavor. A drop on a sugar cube provided a very sweet mouthful and a bit of a sting.

Jean stood up, waved his big arm to the table in general, and bellowed, "Aux vendenges!" ("To the harvest!") We all clambered from the benches and went outside, into the cool morning air. The sky was heavy with cumulus clouds which reached as far as we could see. Going over to the small building behind the house, Jean brought out an armful of black rubber aprons. They were full-length, with a heavy cotton strap to go around the neck and a strap at each side, at the waist, to be tied behind the back. I almost tripped over mine; Jean laughed and found me a smaller one. Wearing our aprons, we followed him for a three-minute walk to the rows of vines we would pick. In days to come, we would be driven, in a small truck, to areas farther away.

We were each given a plastic bucket and a pair of clippers, and were sent in pairs down the rows. Theo and I went together but ended up working far apart. One of the pair was directed to walk to the end of the row, the other to stop about halfway down, the point at which Jean yelled "Arretez!" ("Stop!") The buckets held about two gallons and were carried by a thick metal wire handle. The clippers were the sort with which one would trim a rose bush. We were instructed to clip "seulement les pourris" ("only the rotten ones"). I was surprised, as I had imagined the grapes we would pick would be good ones. They were white—that is, pale green—and many of the clusters had patches of white mold. These were the select grapes, already on their way to natural fermentation, saturated with sugar and converting it to alcohol.

We bent to work where we had stopped, clipping the bunches which were mostly moldy, and dropping them into our buckets. This work was done in a crouched position. When moving on to the next vine, we tended to shuffle over, still bent at the waist and knees. We were to call "un sceau!" ("a bucket!") when a pail was filled. I heard this cry from one of the local pickers and observed that a young Frenchman ran over with an empty pail and traded it for the full one.

He then returned to the end of the rows, where stood a large bin on wheels, towed there by a tractor. He tipped the bucket over the bin, adding the grapes to the small new pile.

Soon, my bucket was full. I called out tentatively for a new one, and he responded. My feeling of accomplishment at having filled a pail vanished, as I gazed into the bottom of the next one. I bent to the task, and shortly cried out for another.

For a while we worked in relative quiet; only our calls for buckets and the rustling of leaves disturbed the gray morning. The leaves and grapes were wet with dew, and muddy from dust of the dry days. Spiders and ants crawled on some of the grapes, but they, along with the dust, went into the bucket. For hours, my eyes were filled with little but visions of large green leaves and small green grapes, with a mottled background of the branches and patches of rich brown earth. Each time I rose to hand over the fruits of my labor and receive another bucket, the scene changed, quickly and briefly. I saw rows of green vines, with curved backs interspersed, and an occasional vertical body. I bent again, studying the clusters and branches, the veins of the leaves, the careful spiders.

After almost two hours had passed, I heard the call for a break. I stood, feeling then how stiff my back had become, and looked around for Theo and Christine. Our eyes rested on each other; we headed over to the large bin, where everyone was gathering. To my amazement, an unlabeled bottle of red wine was being passed around. Whoever reached for it swigged some wine and passed it on to the next outstretched hand. I could hardly believe this: wine in the morning, after two hours of work, with two more to come before lunch! Theo and I laughed and drank along. It was fermented but fresh—the earliest wine of the season. I took my second gulp the next time the bottle came around, and thought it wild fun. Two bottles were consumed by about a dozen of us during the break; not everyone partook in the drinking.

Then we went back to work—back to being dwarfed by twining vines and large flat leaves—as we stooped close to the ground at our labor. It was tiring and routine and slow. It was earthy and quiet and peaceful.

Finally, lunch break came and we gathered by the bin, peering in. It was about half full—a painstaking accomplishment. Everyone seemed to want to talk; we had been silent almost all morning. Walking back to the house together, all were relaxed and chatting. By the outer stone wall, near the kitchen, was a row of hooks. We removed our muddy aprons and hung them to dry. By then there was a light breeze, and the sun was shining between large fluffy clouds.

Lunch was a feast. As on the kibbutz, this meal came after four hours of physical labor, so everyone was hungry. It also had to carry us through four more hours of work on our feet; we ate heartily. There were hard-boiled eggs in one bowl and lettuce salad in another. There were cooked vegetables and boiled potatoes. There was chicken and there was beef. We ate and enjoyed it all (though I resisted the chicken).

After stuffing ourselves sufficiently, we arose at the sweep of Jean's arm to don our rubber aprons and return to the vines. We were willing but slow. Initially the work, on a full stomach, was difficult, but it grew easier. The leaves were dry by then, and there were fewer clouds. A couple of short afternoon breaks were taken, during which a bottle of red wine was again circulated. Theo, Christine, and I worked hard, feeling healthy and happy, aside from some stiffness in our backs. At the end of the workday, we looked with satisfaction at the large wagon being pulled slowly by the tractor. It was brimming with piles of small bunches of grapes.

After walking back to the house, we hung our aprons on the hooks on the rough wall. Jean then asked us to form a line along a small stone building close by. This structure consisted of only one room, about eight feet on a side, with a large wooden door forming one wall. Jean opened this door fully, exposing a stone counter which extended almost the width of the room. There were about a dozen clear glasses, like simple juice glasses, at one end of this counter, along with a corkscrew.

He stepped behind the counter, reached down to some secret spot, and pulled out a bottle of rosé wine. This he held up, in his plump hands, for us to admire. It bore his label, and shone a pale warm pink in the fading afternoon light. Jean removed the cork from the bottle and filled the first glass halfway. He offered it to the nearest person, who accepted it and moved away. Jean then poured the next glass and offered it to the next person in line, who took it and moved on. The ritual continued until each of us had received a glass of the precious rosé. We all stood by the counter, facing Jean on the other side. He poured himself a glass, raised it, and toasted "Santé!"

("Health!"). We all repeated "Santé!" and everyone drank. The wine was sweet and delicious.

So I learned that the red wine was the least expensive, the white the next, and the rosé the prize of this small family vineyard by the Loire. Here was our reward for a good hard day's work, poured with appreciation for each of us by the owner.

After about ten minutes, we went to our rooms to wash and change for dinner. The clanging of the bell almost an hour later announced the meal. It was identical in form to lunch, with two or three appetizers followed by several main dishes and vegetables. I ate rabbit, for the first and only time in my life. (The next day, I saw a large one in a cage in the yard, and suspected it would soon be served for supper. I felt guilty and would not eat rabbit again, though the one I tasted had an enjoyable flavor unlike any meat I had tried before.) This huge meal, consumed with copious amounts of red and white wine, left no room for dessert.

As Jean's wife cleared the table, her husband led the way to an adjacent room. It was large and dark, the old floor and walls all made of wood. To my surprise, Jean picked up an accordion from a bench and began to play. He sang and was joined by several of his neighbors, who apparently were familiar with this performance. It was quite amusing, due to Jean's large size and robust enthusiasm, to see him jump around as he played. Theo and I clapped hands in time, for lack of familiarity with the music, and noticed that everyone was smiling. This scene lasted for about half an hour, after which we departed for our rooms—satiated, delighted, and tired.

The Vineyards—The Departure

Christine left after four days. We thanked her for finding us work there, and promised to write. Her brother—whom we saw rarely—remained, planning a stay of two weeks. Theo and I worked for a few days longer. In mid-October, after seven days, we decided it was time to move on. We had yet to get to Holland, where we wanted to have some time with Theo's family before I flew home in late November. The next day, we told Jean, would be our last.

Weary of the routine but still appreciative of the setting, Theo and I worked as usual. We stuffed ourselves at lunch and planned to leave as soon as the work day ended.

After we returned from the vineyards and had hung up our black rubber aprons for the last time, Jean motioned us over to one of the small stone buildings adjacent to the house. He told us to stick our heads into a small opening cut in one of the white walls. Doing so and looking down in amazement, we saw the 10' x 20' stone floor flooded several feet deep with a clear pink liquid. It was the rosé. One of the workers was reaching through an opening in another wall to set a flexible white vacuum hose down onto the floor beneath the wine. The purpose of this hose, connected to a pump in the next room, was to remove the sludge that settled out during fermentation. This waste was a fine, pinkish-white silt, made of dust from soil and insects and traces of grape skin. At last I understood how our muddy piles of grapes in the bin were transformed into the lovely wine. As they sat and fermented, the impurities slowly filtered down to the white cement floor, little by little, until the wine was aged and clarified to a beautiful, delicious lucidity. The sludge was drawn out and the wine aged further. This process continued until the stone room contained only clear rose, ready to be bottled.

Next, Jean led Theo and me to his office, to pay our wages. Lifting the lid of a small metal box, he checked with us that it had been eight days for each, then withdrew the appropriate amount. Jean counted the francs out as he placed them in our hands, first Theo's, then mine. We realized we owed him some change, and drew out our purses. A quick motion of Jean's heavy arm stopped us.

"J'en ai" (I have some"), he said, pointing to the little metal box. We laughed and thanked him.

He then offered us wine, two bottles each, to take along. Though concerned about carrying the extra weight, we could not refuse his generosity. As we made room in our packs for one bottle of white and one of rosé, Jean's father and wife came to the door to say goodbye. I took out my camera, and we all went outside. They liked the idea of being photographed and willingly posed. We then hoisted our packs onto our backs and left, with thanks and handshakes and smiles.

The Return—I

It took us two days to hitch-hike to the Netherlands. We spent almost no time in Belgium, though we stopped to eat lunch in the tiny country of Luxembourg. By the time we reached Holland, we had consumed one bottle of white wine. The second white and one bottle of rosé would be presented to Theo's parents, while the other rosé was reserved for me to take back to my parents in the States.

When our train pulled into the center of Amsterdam, I had a strange sensation. Theo was in familiar territory and I was not. Through much of our trip, his fluency in German had helped us greatly. He had even been to some of the places we passed through. But this was different, and I felt alien.

Approaching his family's narrow brick house, in a small town close to the city, I felt a bit better. Here was his home, into which I would be welcomed. As his mother opened the door, she smiled and hugged us both and chattered profusely. The fact that I could not understand a word did not interfere with my sense of warmth and relief. His father was less demonstrative, but he shook hands, smiled and seemed glad to see us. Theo led me to a spare bedroom upstairs, probably the one that had been his sister's prior to her marriage. Leaving our packs in our respective rooms, we joined the family downstairs.

Theo acted as translator on many occasions throughout the next two weeks. I met his two brothers, his sister and her husband, and several friends of Theo's from high school, including his old girlfriend. In the evenings with his parents, I was most comfortable. Then, Theo had time to translate, and I quickly picked up many commonly used words and phrases. He had already taught me a bit of Dutch on the kibbutz, and I could occasionally understand a sentence or question from some member of his family.

One day Theo and his younger brother Jan (pronounced Yahn) were talking, in Jan's bedroom, as I sat quietly by. He was the sibling closest in age and temperament to Theo. They had missed each other, and I felt bound to let them enjoy each other's company without frequent requests for translation. Suddenly, from the pieces I had been able to gather, the topic of their conversation became clear to me, and I asked a relevant question. Turning to me with great surprise, Theo exclaimed,

"Your Dutch is getting so good that I can't even have a private conversation with my own brother!" I could see he was pleased, perhaps hoping that my improving comprehension of the language would increase my sense of comfort in his country.

Much of the time we spent visiting his friends, though, I felt handicapped. Theo had not seen these people for a year; he wanted to catch up on their lives and was eager, as well, to share with them his experiences in Israel. It was reassuring to know that I had been there with him, but we were in a different world now. Their conversation was animated and Theo could not be translating as everyone spoke. Somehow, I felt lonely when he enthusiastically related stories about the kibbutz. He had shared experiences with these people also, in the years before we had met; it meant a lot to him to be back with them. And they were clearly pleased to see and listen to him again. I was welcomed, but I was apart.

The Tourists

Free of the weight of our backpacks, we toured Amsterdam for a few days. It was a relief, as well, to be free of deciding where we would sleep each night. Many of the old streets and buildings were quaint, though other portions, including the bustling railway station, made it clear that we were in a large modern city. We took a boat ride on the canals, something Theo would never have done had he not been accompanied by a tourist. Exploring the various faces of Amsterdam was highly enjoyable, though it was very different from any of our other travels.

We decided to do something else that Theo had never done in Amsterdam—visit the Anne Frank house. This was the home in which the family of the twelve-year-old girl who had kept the famous diary had hidden from, and eventually been captured by, the Nazis during World War II. Theo and I had both read her diary and wanted to see the house. We approached it with curiosity and trepidation. It was a house like many others, on a street like many others. Entering an ordinary door, we were shown, along with several other tourists, how the Frank family had been hidden above the living and working space of the obvious part of the building. We were shown through rooms on the first floor, whose walls were lined with black and white photographs of concentration camp victims. The girl's father survived; the rest of the family, and others hiding with them, did not. As we filed past horrible, haunting images, one after another, of people with large, pleading eyes and naked skin stretched tightly over their bones, we struggled to make the connection between them and the calm, common house.

Both of us shaken and crying, we exited the building. Theo had previously expressed his sickened feeling at Nazis having been there, in his country, in his city, so close to his home. He felt awful knowing that they had broken in to take Anne Frank and her family away. We walked slowly until Theo was wracked with sobs. He cried so hard then that we had to stop. Though terribly upset myself, I wondered at his intensity. I put my arms around him and he held me close, cheek on my head. I waited. At last he looked up, exhaled heavily, searching my face, and said softly.

"It could have been you."

The Parting

We both knew that I had to leave soon; neither broached the topic during that first week in Holland. However, since I had to make a flight reservation, we were eventually forced to address it. Possible departure times were discussed, as well as who would drive me to the airport, in the same way that we had previously discussed which town or hostel we should hitch to next. But this time we were separating.

The date was set and the flight reserved. We spent the next few days, the last few days, walking and bicycling around his small village. We spent some of that time with Jan—walking, joking, and taking pictures of each other.

Most of the obligatory visiting was finished by then, but even our time alone together began to feel strange. The distance was already growing.

We planned to be together at the kibbutz the following summer. Beyond that, we had not attempted to decide what would be. I was afraid to leave, feeling we might never see each other again. Theo was back home, and soon I would be, too. Then I would go back to college, after my year's leave. Our life at the kibbutz and our freedom of the previous few months began to seem like a dream.

Theo was more confidant than I that we would meet again in July and plan our future from there. He said he would work in a restaurant and try to save enough money to visit me in the States over the winter.

Of course that would be wonderful, I agreed, though it all seemed unreal and impossible. I felt it was ending.

On a clear fall day, Theo's sister and brother-in-law drove us to the airport. I showed my ticket and passport at the desk, and checked my backpack. Out on the runway, we took pictures of each other as I fought back tears, feeling weak. Theo smiled encouragingly as he accompanied me to the plane, carrying my small day pack. I watched his long legs in their graceful stride, absorbing the familiar image. He handed me my pack. We said goodbye.

The Return—II

For hours, throughout the trip across the dark Atlantic, I cried. Realizing that my sobbing was noticeable, I struggled to be quiet. No one bothered me or tried to console me.

My flight landed safely in Canada, where I had to wait five hours for the connection to New York. Confused and weary, with the sensation of being everywhere and nowhere, I fell asleep on a couch in the terminal.

A few hours later, dawn broke through storm clouds which hung over the runway. There was still plenty of time to make my flight. I found a Women's room, where I washed my face and combed my hair. Sad, bloodshot eyes peered back from the mirror. I wanted to be presentable for my parents.

The flight to New York, on that gray morning in late November, passed uneventfully, except for the fading turmoil in my head. Outside the plane were blue skies and bright sunshine, as we flew above the thick low clouds. I had stopped crying; I was removing myself further every moment, from Theo and the kibbutz and my conflicting emotions about our time together in Holland. Soon, I would return to a university I disliked, in the company of only a few people I cared for. The prospect seemed dull, yet I felt that this was the next step in my life. Perhaps, the following semester, I could transfer out.

Although I had learned that there were other places to be, other lives to be lived, this seemed to be my lot, at that time. I sighed and accepted; Theo and I would write letters. I had exhausted myself on the long flight from Europe; there was almost no emotion left. I grew cold, preparing myself. An imposing stillness took over.

Noting our descent toward the gray clouds, I observed dark wisps against bright blue as we entered the vapor layer, and watched as the grayness swallowed us, masking the sunny space above.

We landed smoothly in a gentle rain. Everything was gray: the runway, the sky, the air.

Down the corridor to the bright waiting area, I marched with the other passengers. My parents were there, and they greeted me with delight. Hugging and smiling, I was glad to see them after such a long time. More than any other emotion, I believe they felt relief on seeing me. My mother commented that I had lost weight; she seemed concerned. The many kilometers I had walked, the energy I had burned, the meals of cheese and bread or yogurt and apples, had slimmed me by ten to fifteen pounds. I had dropped the fat from second servings and extra desserts eaten in dormitory cafeterias out of nervousness and boredom. I was thin; I felt fine.

They were anxious to hear everything. As we walked to the baggage claim area, I tried to answer their questions, but one was often interrupted by another. The backpack I had borrowed for the trip, from Dan in my American kibbutz group, slowly wound its way to me along the curving carousel. I lifted the pack from the belt, but my father insisted on carrying it for me. That was all the luggage I

124

had, except for the small canvas bag I was holding. My parents had received the suitcase sent months earlier, before my European travels began.

Wading through a massive parking lot, we reached the car. I sat quietly in the back as we drove home, gazing uninterestedly out the window at the familiar scenery.

At the sight of the house, I felt a surge of warmth and was glad to see my brother and sister waiting just inside. Both were younger than I, my brother by two years and my sister by five. I imagined they found my travels curious and maybe exciting. They had some general questions, but were mainly just happy to see me again.

I presented my parents with the rosé wine from France, as well as a wooden gingerbread mold I had bought in Amsterdam. They offered me food; I did not want to eat. Filling a large glass with tap water, I drank it down, standing by the sink. I told them that I had eaten on the plane, and that I was tired.

They ushered me to my room, showing me that it had been kept neat and clean for me. I thanked them, kissed them, and closed the door. After pulling the shades, I took off the clothes which I had been wearing for too long, and gratefully lay down in bed. I slept for sixteen hours.

<u>The Conflict</u>

My parents asked a bit about Theo, not really wanting to know. They were glad he was an ocean away, this non-Jewish, non-college-educated, probably irresponsible young man who had encouraged their daughter to do terrible, dangerous, improper things.

Instead, we discussed the kibbutz. They were pleased to hear that I had used my Hebrew in the job at the children's house. It was amusing, they thought, that after so much time spent picking fruit in Israel, I had still wanted to pick grapes in France. Since my parents had been to Paris, we also talked a bit about that city. There were plenty of topics for discussion, as they had also traveled in Israel, a country they found fascinating.

Theo telephoned two days after I returned. My parents were surprised; I wondered whether they were impressed. He told me he'd wanted to call sooner but thought he should give me a chance to recover from the trip. It was exciting to receive his call, though the connection was fuzzy. He said he'd been hired for a restaurant job and would start the following day. As soon as he could save enough money to pay for the flight, he wanted to visit me. I was happy at the prospect but unsure of how it would be with him there. In case classes were starting by the time he arrived, we would go up to school together.

In the meantime, I worked at a temporary sales job in Manhattan; extra help was always needed for the "Holiday Season." When Theo came, we would have that money to spend.

That autumn, I also saw my first serious boyfriend, from high school, a couple of times. Toward the end of our senior year, we had been happy together, and had touched on the beginnings of a physical relationship. Separated a few months later, at universities hundreds of miles apart, problems arose due to minor sexual interactions with others and resulting anger and jealousy on my part. In addition, I was unhappy at college. Although I liked a few of the students in my dormitory, the setting and lack of stimulating atmosphere on campus displeased me. Distraught over Mark and in need of a major change, I had gone to work on a kibbutz. It was something Jewish teenagers were sometimes known to do, and I had a classmate—recently returned—who made it sound like an appealing adventure. My parents, aware of my discomfort, considered it a reasonable way to take a break.

During my time in Israel, I had written to Mark. He had written back more frequently. When I returned, he was still quite interested in me. I'd thought it was over. I had believed that the time apart and my occasional letters about my work and social activities, as well as about Theo, would convince him that I was on my own, without him. They had not.

Mark came to visit; I showed him photographs from my travels. He asked about my life in Israel, about Theo, about my future. Uncertain and confused, I already felt that I had two lives—one on the kibbutz and the one to which I had returned. And now, someone who used to have a strong emotional hold on me was calling for my attention again. Although I could not be unfaithful to Theo, I recognized conflicting desires within myself. Explaining my feelings to my old friend, I did not realize that the admission opened me further to his influence.

The Visitor

In mid-December, Theo called again to say that in two more weeks he would have enough money to fly to New York to be with me. At the start of the new year, he arrived; I was allowed to borrow the car to pick him up at the airport. My eyes scanned the parade of arriving passengers, and there was his blond hair, and then his eyes lighting on me. For a long moment, we held each other tightly, then carried his bag out to the car, unable to stop smiling. It seemed like a very long time since we'd parted at the Netherlands airport, though it had been just six weeks. We told each other about the jobs we'd had; there wasn't much new to relate. It felt good to be together.

Arriving at my parents' house was strange. I was afraid Theo would be treated as an unwelcome curiosity, rather than with the warmth he deserved. My brother and sister were friendly, of course; my father was fairly so. My mother was polite, reserved. Never having never met them before, Theo did not notice this and so was jovial and talkative as ever. We all ate dinner together, except for my brother, who had left that afternoon to return to college. At the table, there was much conversation, and many questions were aimed at Theo. Though he responded to everything in his casual style, I was terribly uncomfortable. Knowing that my parents disapproved, I felt he was being scrutinized. He had anticipated their curiosity, was happy to be conversing, and did not seem to sense what I knew.

Theo was given a room downstairs with a pull-out bed, despite the fact that my brother's room, upstairs near the others, was available. It was judged to be too close to mine. He or we could not be trusted; he had to sleep farther away. For his sake, I tried not to show my annoyance. I went down to help him open the bed and to say goodnight. Theo did not seem to be disturbed about anything, just glad to be there. As he was weary from the flight and time change, I told him that I would look in on him late the next morning.

During the two weeks we spent there, we took several day trips into New York City and also to the beach. It was cold, but we walked and kept warm. Those days were fun and we remained close. Yet a sense of discomfort would not leave me. I felt, somehow, that we were not living in the same world.

Unhappy though I was to admit any twinges other than in his direction, I managed to tell Theo about having seen Mark. I considered not telling him at all, knowing it would disturb him, but thought I should confess. They wanted to meet each other, out of curiosity, interest, or jealousy, perhaps. I agreed and invited a close female friend from high school to join us, in my parents' living room. While I was away, she and I had exchanged letters. She also knew Mark; I thought her presence would help to dampen any tension. That evening, though, there were no problems—just some conversation and a lot of mutual studying of facial features and expressions.

A few days before classes began, Theo and I were driven upstate, by my parents. My freshman-year roommate and a few friends of hers had rented the second floor of a big old house. Denni and I had become friends that first year, and, knowing I was returning, she had informed me that one room was still available in her house. Although I did not know the others well, there was no problem agreeing to rent there or living with them. My bedroom was the smallest, as I had been the last to request a room.

We shared the tiny space, and spent so much time in the kitchen and large living room that the size of the bedroom did not really matter. As it was a bit uncomfortable in the small bed, sleeping was the only problem. We got used to it.

I began my classes on schedule; Theo read novels while I was away. He came to campus with me once or twice, exploring some buildings and the library, but he preferred to be at the house. Sometimes he went grocery shopping during the day then cooked dinner while I studied in the evening at home. Everything was going smoothly. The only trouble was in my head and in the future.

The Concern

Theo must be bored all day, I thought. He claimed he was not. Reading quickly, he finished another novel every few days. Since his visit, as a foreigner, could extend for only three more weeks, I worried about what would come next. How could he remain in the States while I studied? What were our options? We would have to be married, he said, in order for him to get permission from the government to work.

But were we sure? Were we ready? I had always heard—and I believed—that these were questions to be asked when consideration of marriage arose. What would we live on? Theo would be able to obtain only a menial, low-paying job. He would want to go to school. I would not graduate for almost three years; only then would I be able to work and support both of us. It all seemed too difficult; I felt I should not marry him then.

The question of the financing of my college studies, in case I were to be married, had already been brought up. It had been suggested that perhaps the parents were no longer responsible in such a case. If we did marry, and my disapproving parents refused to continue to pay for my education, those three years until graduation would turn into many more. I pictured myself working as a cashier, perhaps, to earn money, while Theo dragged along for many years in some restaurant kitchen. The image was miserable.

I was worried, and I was stubborn. I did not want to live in Israel, on the kibbutz, as Theo suggested. We could both have worked there, maybe even had a room together, until we decided whether or not we wanted to get married. But picking fruit over a long stretch of time would be extremely frustrating, I knew. It seemed time to be back in school. I saw no potentially happy existence for us if we went to live in Holland, either. Theo would probably have to start out at the restaurant, and I would be seeking some similar job.

He tried to comfort me; I was terribly depressed and upset. It seemed impossible to part, yet I saw no way out—no satisfactory resolution. We agreed, again, to go to the kibbutz that summer. Doing that would postpone a final decision. There, we would talk and decide. And it meant time to be together once more, in comfortable territory, though it was five long months away.

Theo's visa ran out; he had to return to the Netherlands. Another student gave us a ride from the university down to my parents'. I knew they were glad to see him leave. I suspected my father liked him; I never knew whether my mother liked him or not. It seemed an irrelevant point.

Driving to the airport, we felt hopeful. As we had met again, once, and had a plan to reunite that summer, this parting was not tearful. Theo would work and save money for the flight to Israel. I would complete that semester's classes. I had some money saved but would need more for the airfare. If my parents would not lend me the rest, I would try to borrow it from friends. We said good-bye, certain that we would meet again. But I was feeling less sure that we could build a future together.

The Doubt

Through the rest of that semester, I concentrated on my studies and wondered what to do the following autumn. I would not remain at the kibbutz past the summer, but I applied to the "Junior Year Abroad" program at the large, reputable university in Jerusalem. My required essay was full of the sense of awe that had overcome me on my first visit to that mesmerizing ancient city. This program was under the aegis of the university I was attending. If accepted, I would be obligated to return there for my senior year. Though my off-campus living situation was pleasant, I did not care to spend more time than was necessary at that school.

At the same time, I applied to spend my Junior year at an Ivy League college in upstate New York. Several of my friends from high school were students there; they all loved it. I felt I should have started out there rather than at the State University at which I was enrolled. An energetic academic atmosphere, a beautiful setting, and the presence of people I had known for years all contributed to my desire to be there. I also knew that if I were accepted for Junior year studies and did well enough, I would probably be able to transfer and graduate from there the following year.

During that spring semester, Mark visited me for a weekend. I had agreed to the suggestion; I wanted to see him too. Emotional uncertainty was peaking then, as I worked diligently through my courses, anticipated the summer at the kibbutz and awaited the responses to my applications for the fall.

Mark arrived on a Saturday morning in March and left on Sunday afternoon. We talked almost constantly, and slept next to each other on the living room floor, sometimes holding each other, even kissing, a bit. Perhaps he gently preyed upon my confusion, drawing on the remnants of my feelings for him, yet I did not feel the relationship held promise. Although we still were close, I could no longer be sufficiently devoted to him. The conflicts of our past—which I supposed I should have forgiven but was unable to do—along with my long-term resentment and jealousy—which I felt to be unhealthy for both of us—the tension of his desire to come together again despite my self-imposed distance, plus the recognition of our non-ideal mesh of personalities had all worn me down. I had talked myself out of it, thought I had extricated myself from it, emotionally and physically.

That weekend, Mark seemed afraid of what would happen when I returned to Israel. He appeared reassured by my uncertainty, the roots of which lay in my capacity to be distracted by and attracted to him. I did not envision a true rekindling of that romance, in case Theo and I decided not to marry. It seemed Mark had more to offer me than I was capable of returning. But my openness to his play on my heart was extremely disturbing. I attributed it to the warmth he and I had shared before I met Theo.

Yet if I could feel drawn to another like this, was my love for Theo not strong enough to last through a lifetime of marriage? Was I too young? Was I too weak? Was Theo not the right one? Were we not right for each other?

The Transition

The spring passed and I worked my way through the semester, eventually receiving high grades in all courses. I had formally decided, as per the required form due to the university by the end of sophomore year, that I would major in English literature. I also enjoyed science and math, continuing to pursue those studies as well, but literature and languages held even greater appeal.

While home life in the large apartment was comfortable, I missed Theo badly. To break up the lonely spell, I had taken a weekend trip, in April, to visit a couple of high school friends at their upstate university and was again impressed with its beauty and atmosphere.

Another weekend that semester, I visited my parents. The family house of Dan, from our American group, was not far from mine. As I still had to return his backpack and retrieve my suitcase, I called to arrange a visit. I learned that he'd already been home once, had returned to the kibbutz for several more months, and was again back in New York. We got together at his house and spent an enjoyable couple of hours talking about Israel. He was enthusiastic about kibbutz life and said he still intended to reside there permanently.

Dan had a surprise for me: he explained that Theo, writing and sending a check from Holland, had requested he purchase a birthday gift for me in Israel. I opened the small box offered to find a silver ring, a type sold in Jerusalem. The jeweler would take a flat band of silver and cut some of it away, leaving letters spelling a Hebrew name. The metal would then be curved to form a ring. Any name could be ordered.

My parents had bought me such a ring a few years earlier, while they were traveling in Israel. I had worn it until it disappeared the previous spring at the kibbutz, from my night table in the little shack. Theo and I could only suspect that a mouse had stolen it. We used to see them scurrying around, though not generally inside the cabins. They had a reputation for liking shiny objects, and it was unimaginable that anyone would have ventured into our shack and taken my ring.

I put the new one on immediately. Dan was glad to see me pleased; I thanked him for his part. On leaving, I remarked that the next time we met might be in Israel. Dan laughed, saying he hoped so.

I needed more money than I had saved from my winter job, for the trans-Atlantic flight I intended to take in June. When asked, my parents agreed to lend me the difference, probably assuming I would otherwise manage to borrow it. We then discussed my summer plans. My father gently suggested that my entire romance with Theo had been a mistake, and that it might not be worth my time and effort (and money) to go to Israel that summer. He received a loud, angry response, in which I informed him that I did not agree with his view of the situation, and that even if he were right, I would never end it with a phone call. I was definitely going.

Europe would be first. The plan was for me to visit with Theo and his family in the Netherlands for a couple of weeks. Then, we would hitch-hike to southern France and fly to Israel from there. That would give us a chance to see the Rhone valley, and flying from Marseilles would be less expensive than flying from Amsterdam.

I bought a backpack—with the help and discount of a friend who found my relationship and travels with Theo terribly romantic, and who had a summer job in a department store—and prepared for my trip. In early June, I departed as planned. My smooth, uneventful flight was met at the airport by Theo and his brother-in-law, the driver. We greeted each other with hugs and smiles; I was excited to be there. I promptly showed Theo my right hand, on which I wore the silver ring he had asked Dan to bring me from Israel. After a short drive to his parents' house, another warm reunion took place.

The next two weeks could not go quickly enough. Theo's parents were pleasant, his brother friendly, his friends still sociable but alien to me. At the kibbutz, I thought, I would feel at home. In the Netherlands, I was uncomfortable and irritable, feeling pressured to decide the future. Relaxation was impossible; I was disturbed, again, by the sensation of my lack of belonging in Theo's world.

One day, we went into Amsterdam and purchased identical summer sleeping bags, to replace our heavier old ones. We walked around a bit and stopped at a small restaurant for lunch. That day was enjoyable; it reminded me of our past travels and those yet ahead. Theo was kind, and happy that I was there. He wanted me to get to know his friends, wanted to relieve my discomfort. He thought my interaction with them would be easier since I was a little more used to hearing Dutch. I wanted to leave.

The Last Chance

After two weeks in the Netherlands, we left for France, packs on our backs. Theo's brother-in-law drove us to a convenient spot that Theo knew, near a highway. We hitch-hiked from there.

Christine wanted us to visit again; we had called ahead to let her know when we might arrive. After several friendly rides and one night in a hostel, Theo and I reached her house. We told her we would stay only one night, in order to have some time in Avignon on our way down the Rhône, followed by two months at the kibbutz.

In the French country house, Theo and I were given the same room as the previous autumn. Setting our packs down, we glanced around at the familiar space. Meanwhile, Christine asked many questions, eager to hear about our travels to date. We happily replied and chatted, glad to be with her again. Theo was anxious, though, and fawned on me a bit, hugging me at random times. Teasing and complaining, Christine said loudly to him (in French),

"But stop hugging her! You have your whole life to hug her!" He dropped his arms then, and looked at me with concern. In the two months ahead, we would have to determine the roles we would play in each others' lives. In fact, the decision rested with me, and I was distracted, often withdrawn. Though Theo tried to pull my emotions to him, I was frequently too remote to respond. At that moment, under Christine's playful, observant gaze, I studied him, uncertain, but tried to smile reassuringly.

"Let's go now," she said.

The puppy from the kibbutz had grown, almost to full size. Taking him along, we walked down small roads, for many kilometers, through the lovely countryside. Tiny flowers of all colors were in bloom, everywhere we looked. The air was fresh and warm, and we were comfortable with Christine.

Her mother, friendly as before, prepared our dinner that night. She was glad to see us and to hear that our French had improved. Afterward, we sat up late, talking with Christine. Theo and I awoke early and prepared our packs. Christine's mother had left for work even earlier, so we parted with regards and thanks to her. After hugging Christine, kissing her on both cheeks, and patting the dog, we set out.

Since it was almost summer, Theo had bought a light tent for our trip along the charming Rhône valley. We spent a few days in Avignon, sleeping at a camping area on a hill just outside the city. Other than in Israel, I had never been in such an old city; we were surrounded by darkened stone buildings with orange-tiled roofs. It felt good to be traveling to new places and sight-seeing together again.

When we reached the mouth of the Rhône—a huge, flat expanse—we camped by a very small town. On a deep, extensive beach, we set up our tent near several others. The air was warm, the sky clear azure. The sun was bright all day. To the east lay the wealthy resort cities of the Riviera; to the west lay some French towns with bull-fighting rings, due to their proximity to Spain. We remained on the lulling Mediterranean beach in between for several days.

We spent them walking in the sand, conversing with a few other travelers, and spending the hot mid-day drinking cold crème-de-menthe with water—a popular local custom—under the large flat straw roof of a nearby restaurant. Around noon each day, people would gather at this one commercial spot on the quiet beach. Locals and tourists slowly wandered over, across the sand, until almost every small table was occupied. We all sat—sometimes for hours—sipping cool emerald green drinks, at our leisure. We let the sun follow its course a bit lower before venturing out again, refreshed, into the wearying heat. Then Theo and I would wander the beach or sit and talk, until it was time to eat our dinner (consisting of whatever we had packed) and slide, in the dark, into our sleeping bags.

After a few days of this life, it was time to go. We had reserved seats on a flight from Marseilles. From our peaceful beach village, we hitch-hiked into the city, then took a taxi to the airport.

During the flight to Tel Aviv, we talked about the visit with Christine and what we had seen of France. Throughout those days in Europe, our interaction had been somewhat testy—I on edge and Theo nervous. It was a relief to be on the way to the kibbutz. There, people knew me, and I would be able to relax. The tension of my reliance on Theo, felt most strongly in the Netherlands, would fade further, and I would be able to speak for myself, be myself. I looked forward to that independence.

Our flight arrived on time. From the airport, we took a bus south, to the desert, scanning the countryside for familiar views as we rode. We studied each other without speaking, considering what it meant to be there. This was the place where we had met; it would give us time, a hiatus from the western world and our structured pasts. This was the place that could bring us together, the place in which we had to decide.

The Distance

When we arrived at the kibbutz, Theo stepped out of the bus and onto the dusty earth first, extending an arm to help me down. It was so familiar, yet strange too, after ten months away. I turned my head to encompass the scene once again. Across the road and dry waving land, I could make out the tents of the Bedouin village. A few paces ahead of us stood the cyclone fence of the kibbutz, topped with barbed wire.

We went to the gate and waited there for Benny the guard to let us in. He came forward, hesitated, then recognized us with a smile. During our months there, we had talked with him quite a bit and become friendly. Opening the gate, he asked how we had been, welcoming us in his limited English. Theo and I recalled the night, early on in our previous stay, when Benny had taken us out in the Jeep for his midnight rounds of the perimeter of the kibbutz. The political situation had been so quiet then; no danger at all, just fun and joking that night with him, and Theo's arm around my shoulders.

We walked up the path to see Reuben and to find out where we would be staying. Grinning, as ever, he welcomed us. As he explained that there was not enough space for us to have our own room, he seemed rather apologetic. Although the kibbutzniks had been expecting us, there were many volunteers that summer. Most rooms had three volunteers of the same sex. If they gave us a room together, there would be one less bed available for another volunteer.

145

The shacks, which housed only two, were all occupied. I accepted the news with a bit of sadness and a bit of relief, realizing my ambivalence and sense of pressure about the future. Theo accepted it also, but asked when there might be more space. Reuben did not know. He showed us to our respective rooms and introduced us to our new roommates in the U-shaped Ulpan we remembered so well.

Theo and I settled into the work routine, most days assigned to different locations. We always ate dinner together, though we did not always enter the dining hall with hands held and big smiles, as we had the previous year.

Each Shabbat, we visited our kibbutz families and joined them for dinner. Both were delighted to have us back, making us feel truly at home. From our kibbutz brothers and sisters, we learned that one kibbutz soldier had been wounded in the October conflict. He was paralyzed from the waist down, a tragedy felt by all the members. We did not know him, as he had been away at the army through most of our previous stay. Each day now, we saw him in his wheelchair at the back of the dining hall. Other than that, little had changed with the members.

Most of the other volunteers were new to us, but we soon became friendly with several of them. As I did not intend to stay for too long, however, my approach was a bit less open than it had been before.

In addition to chatting and letter-writing at the Ulpan, relaxing by the swimming pool was a favorite summer afternoon activity. After work, everyone went to the pool—members, children, and volunteers. The water temperature was not much below that of the air but was sufficiently refreshing. Mara—who was happy to have Theo and me back at the kibbutz—still impressed us with her dives.

Although Theo and I spent our free time together, most working hours were spent apart. Once in a while, a particular fruit would be ripening and require as many volunteers as possible for a few days or even a week. Then Theo and I worked side by side, and ate all our meals together. On those occasions, we were both glad for the proximity. But usually, he was assigned to the refet, to work with the cows, and I to pick fruit or work in the gardens.

The Pressure

Two weeks after our arrival in Israel, my parents called to inform me that both of my Junior year study applications, to the university in Jerusalem and to the one in upstate New York, had been accepted. They were pleased to be able to pass this information on to me and said that they, as well as both universities, awaited my response. Of course, they acknowledged, I would have to think about it for a while. I was told that a daughter of a friend of theirs had attended that Jerusalem university and had had to take a bus from her dormitory to classes. This was presented as information to be weighed in the negative when considering that option. The fact that I had lived, for two years, three miles from the main state university campus, first in dormitories and then in a shared house, necessitating bicycle or bus transportation, was not noted. My parents asked how I was doing; I answered vaguely. The call was expensive and the connection a bit weak, so we kept the conversation short. They said they would look forward to hearing from me as soon as possible.

At the end of the workday, I told Theo what had happened. He was so glad I could spend a year in Jerusalem and hoped I would. I told him I wondered how much we would be able to see each other if I were there—weekends, certainly, though he would have to work on Sundays, and I would undoubtedly have classwork and exam preparation to do even on his days off. Also, the thought of starting out there was a bit intimidating. Though Jerusalem was wonderful and, to some extent, familiar, becoming a student at the university would certainly require a major adjustment. While I loved the city, I felt I had done enough exploring for a while. Had I not spent so much of the previous year traveling in Israel, I might have been more enthusiastic. Gradually, almost unconsciously, I came to feel that I wanted to go home.

The main point of studying in Jerusalem would be to give Theo and me a chance. But I planned to study English literature, and knew very well that Israel was not the ideal place for that. In addition, Theo and the kibbutz would be a one-and-a-half hour bus ride away. When I brought up the possibility of my attending the university in New York state, he became defensive. Why would I go there? We would be apart again, possibly able to visit for a few weeks during the winter again, then apart until the summer. It was likely to doom the relationship. I admitted it.

Neither situation was satisfactory; I didn't know what to do. The one imperative, for many reasons, was that I continue with my studies and graduate. I had friends at the ivy league school in upstate New York and could probably do well enough to stay there for my senior year. Both times I'd visited, I had been comfortable in that environment. In Jerusalem, I knew no one. Theo and I would be able to spend a maximum of one day together each week, and not even every week. Also, the year following my junior year abroad—if I chose that route—would present me again with the problem of separating from him or marrying him, as well as returning to a university at which I had not been happy.

Theo worried, debated, and waited. I agonized, knowing the choice was mine.

My parents called again, and again, to ask what I would do. Their effort involved calling the central phone, preferably at mealtime, and waiting while someone went to find me and I walked over to the telephone office. Our calls were tense. They were pressing; I was resisting, all the while susceptible and sliding, having been raised "a good girl", all the while unsure of what was right. They wanted me back; they wanted me away from Theo. I had shocked them by refusing to return directly from Israel the previous year, instead traveling around Europe with someone they could not imagine. I wanted them to approve of my life partner; I did not want to be arguing and miserable. But Theo had been so good for me; he loved me and inspired love in me. In many respects, he had expanded my horizons. He stood by me; he wanted to stay with me, and I with him. I resented my parents' pressure, and felt more and more hopeless.

After each telephone call, I discussed the conversation with Theo. We consoled each other, at the precipice of a major event in our lives. Whichever way it went, it frightened me. There would be a big family wedding, or so I'd always thought, when I married. There would be relatives offering gifts to help start our new life, our new lives. Everyone would be happy for me, or so I'd imagined. Now my parents were disapproving, my mother threatening to withdraw college funding, my father attempting to convince me that my head had been in the clouds, that Theo was not for me.

Was I being bought? Could I be susceptible to financial pressure? I had never concerned myself with money; my parents had supplied what was needed and I never wanted more. We lived in a fairly affluent neighborhood, but I never had much jewelry or fancy clothes, nor did I crave them. Although my tuition and necessary college expenses were paid by my parents—a luxury for some others, I realized—I had worked summer jobs in order to have spending money. On the kibbutz, we worked and were given what we needed, with tickets offered to buy treats once each week in their small store. It was plenty for me.

Theo and I had lived with little money; it had never worried me. When Theo's ran out, in Europe, we spent what was left of mine. We were both willing to work for more, when needed, and spend less, when necessary. Of course, we would eventually need more for the future, but that would come in time. No, I could not believe that I was too materialistic.

Yet the emotional pressure weighed on me. I was quite upset by my parents' attitude. Didn't I know what was best for myself? Had they had their way, I never would have traveled through Europe as I had with Theo. The development of this intimate, encompassing relationship would not have continued, and I would have missed a huge, rich, and important chapter of my existence.

On the other hand, I was extremely concerned with the life Theo and I could have together. Staying at the kibbutz permanently was out of the question; picking fruit with no end in sight would drive me out of my mind. I also feared I might resent him for keeping me

151

there. Getting married and going to the States together, if I were a student, meant a low-level, boring job for Theo, which he claimed he would not mind. He had been wonderful during that month in upstate New York, but wouldn't it be much harder on him over two years? And what if my parents did indeed refuse to fund the remainder of my schooling? Then we would both have to find what would undoubtedly be unsatisfying jobs and save money for many more than two years before we could take turns at extending our educations and finding more challenging and rewarding work. It looked bleak. In addition, I was afraid I was not ready to commit to marriage.

I continued to weigh the other two possibilities; going to Jerusalem for a year, going back to New York state alone. Tormented by questions and doubts, I cringed as Theo's eyes begged. I didn't want to leave him, didn't want to stay. Maybe I just wanted to go home, but not to my parents' home. The kibbutz was like home, but one that seemed not to offer long-term satisfaction. Putting myself in a dissatisfying position to stay with Theo would lead to an unhappy relationship, I believed. Perhaps I was ignorant in that regard. Had I married him, stayed on the kibbutz, and become a member, I might have been offered more challenging jobs, eventually, involving greater responsibility. At the time, though, I was faced with the prospect of years ahead spent looking at blue sky through thousands and thousands of endless green leaves.

The Decision

Some days that summer, we began work at four in the morning, riding out to the potato fields to hoe weeds. The tractor pulled us in for breakfast, then back out for two more hours. It was necessary to start early, under a dark sky and shining moon, so that we could finish at ten-thirty. After that, the sun was too intense, the heat too brutal, for unshaded work.

One of the volunteers who had recently arrived was a young French woman, about our age, called Nana. She and I hoed side by side in the potato fields and often sat together, chatting in French, by the pool. Nana was Jewish and had traveled to Israel alone—as an adventure. Working on a kibbutz, she had decided, would allow her to explore while earning her keep. Her name was actually Nanette, she confided to me and Theo, which she found intolerable.

While writing letters at the Ulpan, I would observe her waist-length, untrimmed wavy brown hair—never constrained by any sort of band or clip—with thin ends fluttering in the occasional breeze. She wore loose, gauzy cotton dresses which hung down to her ankles and swayed as she ambled to the dining hall for dinner. As she spoke no English, she tended toward those who could speak French. I enjoyed her calm—rather dreamy—and open personality, as did Theo. We three began spending more and more time together.

It became apparent to me, as well as to Theo, that Nana found him attractive. In conversation, she would rest her eyes on his—prepared to wait forever, it seemed, for his gaze to focus on her. She would play with a few blades of grass while we sat by the Ulpan then suddenly tilt her head coyly toward him with a subtle smile, in an attempt to gain and hold his attention. Though Nana was never aggressive, her feelings were clear. I knew Theo recognized them; he did not show it.

After an hour of dancing at the Moadon one Shabbat, I left to go to sleep. I did not want to miss the rest of the party, but I was very tired. Theo and I were no longer inseparable, though of course I said good-night. He wanted to stay. The next day, he told me that Nana, with whom he had danced quite a bit, had demonstrated some interest in him. I had nothing to ask or say. The following Shabbat, I again went to bed early. In the morning, he told me that he and Nana had danced. He admitted that after leaving the Moadon this time, they had kissed. Although Theo was disturbed over the confession of his behavior, I felt ambivalent—oddly relieved that he would have someone at the kibbutz if I were no longer there.

But his response to her was short-lived; I had known he did not truly care. Perhaps he was being desperate in moving toward her; perhaps he was even doing something he thought I might want. Once his attitude cooled, an angry Nana accused him of having toyed with her. Though that had not been his intention—and though he had probably not given their interaction very much attention at all—he offered no rebuttal or excuse. (Always friendly to me, Nana later said that she had seen, in us, a very unhappy couple and had found no reason not to pursue Theo).

For my part, I was forced to assume full guilt, if I abandoned him. No one else's presence or interest would diminish that. Theo's fascination with and subsequent rejection of Nana was, to my mind, a backdrop for the larger drama.

I was inundated with possibilities and pressure. As the days passed, Theo and I grew disturbed and irritable. In his desire, he was a source of pressure, too. All I saw then, though, was his sensitivity and my potential to injure him.

Betty, from our American group, was still at the kibbutz—by then, quite settled in. Her relationship with the handsome blond kibbutznik continued to make her happy; they still planned to marry. Though she and I saw little of each other that summer—partly due to her free time being spent with Adam, partly because she worked every day with the cows and I never did—I knew her well, thanks to our previous months together. As Theo worked in the refet also, they had become good friends. I therefore decided to discuss my situation, including the difficulty and necessity of making a decision, with Betty. She considered the problem, briefly, and responded,

"Well, Theo is your home. So it doesn't really matter where you live." I thanked her, though it did not seem so clear and simple to me.

The consequences of any action I might take worried me. Any way I turned, someone would be hurt and upset, by me. I was afraid to commit to marriage due to personal doubts and parental pressure. I was afraid to stay and end up resentful of our relationship. What would be safest? The answer seemed to be leaving and going to a different college in New York state. My few female friends there would form a new basis for contact; the environment would be comfortable, beautiful, and academically challenging.

I was miserable. Parting from Theo was not what I wanted. My desire was to prolong the life we'd had, to go back to our earlier volunteer days with eager months ahead, to revert to backpacking in Europe with time, still, before my airline ticket ran out. But it was gone, and impossible; the seasons pressed on. In the end, I decided to leave.

The leaps of mind and action it would have taken to overcome it all were not within my power—not then, maybe not ever. I imagine we could have married, remained on the kibbutz, and asked if I could attend university (though it would have taken years before that would have had a chance of coming about). Or we could have married and gone to live in the Netherlands. There, I could have worked while he attended school, if that were financially possible. Maybe we would have lived with his parents. Then, several years later, I could have had my turn at further education while he supported us. Or else, we could have married and gone back to the States, then found out whether my parents really would have refused to pay for the rest of my college years.

Ah…but I had not the perspective, the nerve, or the will for any of those. So I chose to continue my education in a desirable environment, one in which I intended to remain for my senior year. My parents were, of course, quite pleased with my decision. Theo was depressed but tried to be supportive. And though having made the decision offered some relief, my own emotions were in turmoil.

Theo and I were sad, very sad. Was I doing a good thing? I couldn't tell; I could hardly think anymore.

Maybe we would see each other during my winter break, we half-heartedly said, or at least the next summer. Hope was slim, though, as neither would have the money to fly.

On the scheduled August day, one of the kibbutzniks gave us a ride to the Tel Aviv airport. Theo walked me out to the runway and handed me my small pack which he'd been carrying. Hugging and crying, we assured each other that we would write. I left.

<u>The Memory—I</u>

Theo remained at the kibbutz, planning to work through the fall and winter then return to the Netherlands the following spring. That did not happen, however, due to his relationship with our Israeli friend Mara. We had both known that she was fond of him. I used to wonder whether all the time she spent with the volunteers, including romances with a few of the young men, was due to a wish that one of them would fall in love with her and take her away. In any case, she was there for Theo after I left.

Within a few months of my departure, Mara was pregnant. She wanted to keep both the baby and Theo; he would not desert her. They flew to the Netherlands to introduce her to his family and to be married, in an informal civil ceremony. They then went back to the kibbutz, where a big party was given for them, in the members' Moadon.

All this, Theo wrote to me. He sent pictures of them in Holland, petite Mara large near the end of her pregnancy. We corresponded for a few years, until he became too annoyed with my lack of direction in determining my future—partner, location, career. In one of his last letters, he enclosed a photo (which he had taken, then developed and printed in the kibbutz darkroom) of their year-old baby. My hand trembled as I held it and stared at the light, sharp eyes, the fine, pale hair, the long, thin fingers—unusual for a baby—the image so like Theo in miniature.

Back in the States, I pursued my bachelor's degree in English literature. I thrived academically, was happy socially, and, in my first few days there, met someone with whom I would become romantically involved. After graduation, I moved with him to California, where I went on to study chemistry. Eventually, I knew he was not the person I would marry. All this I wrote to Theo.

Three years after leaving Israel, I was no longer with the man with whom I'd moved west, though I remained in California, working as a chemist. There, living in a shared house perched on a scenic hillside near the edge of the Pacific, I received Theo's last letter. His frustration with me was clear. I replied, anyway, but received no response.

One nostalgic day two years after that, sitting pensively on the deck, I wrote him the following, never to be sent:

As the long afternoon light gradually dims, I watch the wild grasses bow up and down across the ravine. They whisper, the trees rustle, and the air brings me a scent that we used to know in a place far away. Many feelings and thoughts have come and passed since I was there, but do not think that I have forgotten.

Every day you still see the images that lie in my mind; you feel the strong sun through the clear air and see the endless fields and dry hills that I remember. The dark pines and eucalyptus separating the orchards from the fields are not gone from my recall. And the

159

straw-colored grass that I see here in the ravine, gradually turning green with the winter and spring rains, is familiar.

Only the sunset will never be the same, never as red as there, nor the graying evening, like the one that faded into dusk and nothingness when we and the dusty road seemed to follow.

Alone in the clarity of daylight, I remember that evening. This new place does not grow strange; it is home now. You are home now too, a continent, an ocean, and a sea away, in a land I also know. The grass here is not so different from there, nor the dark pines and eucalyptus trees, nor the smell of the air. And though years have gone by, neither are we.

The Memory—II

Two years later, I sit in a house near Boston, Massachusetts. I hold an interesting and challenging job in a research laboratory at a highly respected institution. Prior to this, I had an apartment to myself for over a year, closer to downtown. It is preferable, for now, to share a house. At the moment, no one else is home. I am sipping dry white wine—French—and listening to Haydn on my stereo, feeling very much alone.

I am recently recovered from a brief relationship. He was becoming more involved with me than he cared to be with anyone, despite our many enjoyable times and easy interaction, so he ended it after nine months together. I recall something deeper.

Theo's first child must be five years old by now. He has another son, two or three years younger. I wonder if they are healthy and if there are any more children.

He may have been given other responsibilities at the kibbutz, but I still imagine him doing the same job he used to do: weighing the bulls to see which should be sold for meat, and driving the tractor while some volunteer pushes bales of green hay off the back to feed the cows. He must still go back to his white apartment house set on a green lawn, in his black rubber boots and blue work clothes, sweaty and dusty, spattered with cow dung. He used to come home to our shack like that. Seeing me waiting, he would smile as he walked up the dusty hill, then give me a big hug. He liked to hug me right when he came back from work, covered with splotches of manure, because I would always squeal.

What wouldn't I give now for such a friend and lover who had that much room in his life for me? But I made the decision for us. Could I have done anything else at the time and still claimed rationality? Should rationality have been of primary importance in that choice?

I have considered many times since, at various stages and locations of my life, how we would have fared together, often thinking how well he would have fit in with a certain group of friends of mine, how much he would have enjoyed a certain moment, a certain environment, or how much better he would have been for my heart and mind than some others I later knew.

Haydn's symphony is background for gazing into my crystal ball of a hypothetical past—a pointless activity, I suppose. My glance falls on my right hand. I am wearing the ring he gave me for my twentieth birthday, my Hebrew name cut in the silver band, the flesh of my finger showing between the letters. I treasure it.

CPSIA information can be obtained at www.ICGtesting.com
Printed in the USA
266573BV00001B/21/A